Bilal SGUIRI
Faiq GMIRA
Salwa HABIBY

APPLIED ARTIFICIAL INTELLIGENCE AND MACHINE LEARNING

Bilal SGUIRI
Faiq GMIRA
Salwa HABIBY

APPLIED ARTIFICIAL INTELLIGENCE AND MACHINE LEARNING

PREDICTING AND OPTIMIZING CLICK RATES ON WEB ADVERTISEMENTS #Implementation in Python

ScienciaScripts

Cover image: www.ingimage.com

This book is a translation from the original published under ISBN 978-620-7-47948-1.

Publisher:
Sciencia Scripts
is a trademark of
Dodo Books Indian Ocean Ltd. and OmniScriptum S.R.L publishing group

120 High Road, East Finchley, London, N2 9ED, United Kingdom
Str. Armeneasca 28/1, office 1, Chisinau MD-2012, Republic of Moldova, Europe
Printed at: see last page
ISBN: 978-620-8-19557-1

ARTIFICIAL INTELLIGENCE AND MACHINE LEARNING APPLIED TO DIGITAL MARKETING :

PREDICTION AND OPTIMIZATION

CLICK-THROUGH RATES ON WEB ADS

#Python implementation

Directed by :

- ***Bilal SGUIRI***
- ***Faiq GMIRA***
- ***Salwa HABIBY***

One of our big goals in search is to make it really understand exactly what you want, to understand everything in the world. As computer scientists, we call this artificial intelligence.

Larry Page

SUMMARY

In this book, we first explore artificial intelligence, which enables us to create machines that function and react like humans. Secondly, we use it and its sub-domain of machine learning to achieve general optimization of digital marketing performance, and in particular to improve customer engagement.

With the aim of improving customer engagement, we design and implement hyper-personalized experiences to automate the complex tasks involved in predicting consumer behavior. To achieve this, machine learning is used to perform granular customer segmentation, dynamic content adaptation, precise product recommendations and predictive analysis to anticipate customer needs.

For data collection, we leverage AI-assisted Chatbots coupled with real-time sentiment analysis to improve marketing customer engagement. This is achieved through data analysis, multi-variate testing, attribution modeling and predictive optimization.

However, the book objectively discusses the importance of ethical and responsible use to avoid the potential risks associated with machine learning, such as the echo chamber effect and dead Internet theory.

This book contains a practical realization, which deals with a case study for predicting clicks on advertisements. This practical realization validates the added value of machine learning for optimizing marketing strategies.

All the approaches proposed in this book are programmed using the Python language and its machine learning libraries: Pandas, NumPy, Matplotlib and Scikit-learn.

Keywords: Artificial intelligence; Machine learning; Regression; Prediction, digital marketing; Python; Pandas; NumPy; Matplotlib; Scikit-learn.

CONTENTS

GENERAL INTRODUCTION

In the digital age, digital marketing has established itself as an essential pillar of business strategy. However, the rapid evolution of technology and consumer behavior poses a constant challenge to marketers. How can we capture the attention of an increasingly demanding public? How can messages be personalized to reach each individual in a relevant way? How can marketing campaigns be optimized to maximize their impact and return on investment?

Artificial intelligence, and machine learning in particular, offers a promising solution to these challenges. By harnessing the power of algorithms and the analysis of massive data. Machine learning offers marketers unprecedented tools for understanding, anticipating and influencing consumer behavior. From ultra-precise customer segmentation to the automation of repetitive tasks, the personalization of offers and the prediction of trends, machine learning is revolutionizing digital marketing practices.

However, the integration of machine learning into digital marketing also raises crucial questions. How can we guarantee the ethics and transparency of these algorithms? How can bias and discrimination be avoided? How can we preserve consumers' privacy while exploiting their data?

In this book, we'll explore the synergies between these two powerful fields, namely: digital marketing and machine learning, paving the way for more targeted, personalized and effective marketing strategies. In a case study in this book, we'll start by introducing the conceptual foundations by defining key concepts and tracing their historical evolution, from the theoretical underpinnings of online marketing to recent breakthroughs, whether through renouncement or profound.

After laying these theoretical foundations, we'll explore the different types of digital marketing and machine learning in depth, highlighting their respective advantages, disadvantages and applications. Armed with this in-depth understanding, we'll then look at the practical applications of integrating these two fields, exploring how machine learning algorithms can be harnessed to optimize digital marketing campaigns.

We'll highlight the tangible benefits of this synergy, including a better understanding of consumer behavior, more relevant communication and optimized marketing spend. We'll focus on a crucial use case: predicting clicks on online ads, by building and training a machine learning model using tools such as Python, Pandas, NumPy, Matplotlib and Scikit-learn.

Finally, we'll analyze the results obtained and their practical implications in depth, highlighting the potential benefits of integrating machine learning into digital marketing strategies to optimize advertising campaigns, maximize revenue and improve overall performance.

ARTIFICIAL INTELLIGENCE AND MACHINE LEARNING

CHAPTER I :

► ARTIFICIAL INTELLIGENCE AND MACHINE LEARNING

1.1 Introduction

In this chapter, we'll explore the essential foundations of artificial intelligence and machine learning, starting with an in-depth definition of these concepts and an overview of their historical development. Artificial intelligence, which encompasses a variety of fields such as machine learning, natural language processing and robotics, has transformed the way machines interact with the world and solve complex problems.

We then look in detail at the different types of machine learning, focusing on supervised, unsupervised and reinforcement learning. We will analyze their distinctive features, their advantages and their specific applications in various contexts.

After laying these conceptual foundations, we'll turn our attention to the essential algorithms and techniques of machine learning. We will explore a range of approaches, such as regression, classification, clustering and dimensionality reduction, which enable AI systems to analyze data and make decisions. We will also examine the fundamental concepts of neural networks and deep learning, and their crucial role in recent advances in AI.

This chapter aims to provide a comprehensive understanding of the key concepts, paradigms and techniques of artificial intelligence and machine learning, laying the foundations for further exploration of their practical application in various fields of science and technology.

In this chapter, we'll explore the essential foundations of artificial intelligence and machine learning, starting with an in-depth definition of these concepts and an overview of their historical development. Artificial intelligence, which encompasses a variety of fields such as machine learning, natural language processing and robotics, has transformed the way machines interact with the world and solve complex problems.

We then look in detail at the different types of machine learning, focusing on supervised, unsupervised and reinforcement learning. We will analyze their distinctive features, their advantages and their specific applications in various contexts.

1.2 Artificial intelligence

1.2.1 The foundations

Artificial Intelligence (AI)[1] is a vast and evolving field of computer science that focuses on the creation of intelligent agents, which are systems capable of reasoning, learning and acting autonomously. AI research has made significant progress in developing effective techniques for solving a wide range of problems, from strategic gaming to complex medical diagnostics. At its core, AI aims to reproduce or simulate human intelligence in machines, enabling them to perform tasks that typically require human cognitive abilities. These tasks include understanding and processing natural language, recognizing complex patterns in data, making informed decisions based on available information, and even demonstrating a degree of creativity to generate new solutions or artistic expressions.

The overriding goals of AI research are ambitious and far-reaching, going beyond the simple automation of tasks. They encompass the creation of systems capable not only of performing specific tasks with human-level competence, but also of demonstrating a deeper understanding of the world around them, their

Enabling us to reason, learn and adapt in ways that were once considered the exclusive domain... of human intelligence. Of human intelligence. Some of the key objectives of AI include:

[1][1]David L. P., Alan K. M. (2023), "Artificial Intelligence: Foundations of Computational Agents", "1.1 what is artificial intelligence?", 3rd edition. https://artint.info/3e/html/ArtInt3e.Ch1.S1.html

1.2.1.1 Problem solving

AI aims to develop algorithms and techniques capable of efficiently solving complex problems in a variety of fields. This includes optimizing logistics and supply chains, designing new drugs and materials with desired properties, and even solving global challenges such as climate change and epidemics. AI's problem-solving capabilities have the potential to revolutionize industries and improve our daily lives by finding innovative solutions to complex problems that were previously unsolvable.

1.2.1.2 Knowledge representation

One of the central aims of AI is to create efficient ways of representing knowledge and information in a format that machines can understand and reason with. This involves developing formalisms and structures to represent facts, relationships, uncertainties and even abstract concepts. By enabling AI systems to store and manipulate knowledge in a structured way, researchers aim to create machines capable of reasoning logically, drawing conclusions and making informed decisions on the basis of the information available to them.

1.2.1.3 Learning

AI strives to create systems capable of learning from data and experience, continually improving their performance over time without the need for explicit programming. Machine learning algorithms, the cornerstone of AI, are designed to identify patterns, generalize from examples and adapt to new situations. This ability to learn from data is crucial for tasks such as image recognition, natural language processing and autonomous decision-making, where rules and models may be too complex to be explicitly programmed.

1.2.1.4 Perception

AI research aims to equip machines with the ability to perceive and interpret sensory data from the world around them. This includes the development of computer vision systems capable of analyzing images and videos, recognizing objects, faces and even emotions. In addition, AI is being used to develop speech recognition systems capable of transcribing spoken language into text, enabling voice commands and interactions with devices. The aim is to create AI systems capable of perceiving and understanding the world in a similar way to humans, enabling them to interact more effectively with their environment.

1.2.1.5 Robotics

AI plays a crucial role in the development of intelligent robots capable of interacting with the physical world, performing tasks autonomously and collaborating with humans. This involves integrating AI algorithms with robotic hardware to create systems capable of navigating complex environments, manipulating objects with precision and much more. and learning new skills through trial and error. AI-based robots have the potential to revolutionize sectors such as manufacturing, healthcare and logistics, as well as assisting humans with dangerous, repetitive or high-precision tasks.

1.2.2 The concepts

The foundation of artificial intelligence[2] rests on two fundamental concepts: intelligence and cognition, and problem solving and knowledge representation. These concepts are closely related and essential to understanding how AI systems work and achieve their goals.

1.2.2.1 Intelligence and cognition

Intelligence, in the context of AI, refers to a system's ability to reason, learn and adapt to new situations. It encompasses a wide range of cognitive abilities, such as problem-solving, decision-making, perception, language comprehension and even creativity. AI research aims to understand the underlying mechanisms of intelligence and reproduce them in machines, enabling them to perform tasks once thought to be the exclusive domain of humans. This involves studying how humans think, learn and solve problems, then translating this information into algorithms and computer models that can be implemented in AI systems.

---

[2][2] David L. P., Alan K. M. (2023), "Artificial Intelligence: Foundations of Computational Agents", "1.4 Prototypical Applications", 3rd edition. https://artint.info/3e/html/ArtInt3e.Ch1.S4.html

Cognition, on the other hand, refers to the mental processes involved in acquiring knowledge and understanding, including thinking, reasoning, memorizing and problem-solving. AI research in cognition aims to develop models and algorithms capable of simulating these mental processes, enabling machines to process information, make inferences and generate new knowledge. This involves exploring areas such as knowledge representation, reasoning under uncertainty and cognitive architectures capable of handling complex cognitive tasks.

1.2.2.2 Problem solving

Problem solving is a fundamental aspect of AI, and involves finding solutions to complex problems using a systematic approach. AI systems use various techniques, such as search algorithms, heuristics and logical reasoning, to explore the space of possible solutions and identify the optimal solution. Search algorithms systematically explore the solution space, evaluating different options and selecting the most promising ones on the basis of predefined criteria. Heuristics are rules of thumb or shortcuts that can guide the search process, making it more efficient. Logical reasoning enables AI systems to deduce new information from existing knowledge, enabling them to solve problems requiring logical deduction and inference.

1.2.2.3 Knowledge representation

Knowledge representation is another crucial AI concept, as it concerns the way in which information is stored and organized within an AI system. This involves developing formalisms to represent facts, relationships and uncertainties, enabling AI systems to reason about the world and make informed decisions. Knowledge representation techniques include semantic networks, which represent knowledge as a graph of interconnected concepts, and ontologies, which define the relationships between concepts and their properties. By representing knowledge in a structured, machine-readable format, AI systems can access and manipulate information, draw conclusions and make decisions based on their knowledge base.

1.2.3 Categories and approaches

1.2.3.1 Types of artificial intelligence systems

1.2.3.1.1 Narrow and general artificial intelligence

Artificial intelligence systems[3] can be broadly classified into two main types: narrow AI and general AI.

Narrow AI (ANI), also known as weak AI, refers to AI systems designed and trained to perform specific tasks. These systems excel in designated areas, but lack the ability to generalize their knowledge or skills to other domains. Examples of Narrow AI include image recognition software, language translators, spam filters and recommendation systems. Although Narrow AI has enjoyed remarkable success in recent years, it operates within predefined limits and lacks the vast cognitive capabilities of humans. It relies on specialized algorithms and models tailored to the specific task at hand, making it highly efficient and accurate within its limited scope. However, narrow AI systems cannot perform tasks outside their programmed domain, and require human intervention to adapt to new situations or challenges.

General AI (AGI), also known as strong AI, represents hypothetical AI systems with human-like intelligence, capable of understanding, learning and applying their knowledge in a wide range of tasks. AGI would be able to reason, solve problems and make decisions in new and complex situations, much like a human being. It would exhibit cognitive abilities such as abstract thinking, creativity and the ability to transfer knowledge from one domain to another. However, the realization of the AGI remains a major challenge in AI research, and its realization remains a subject of ongoing debate and speculation. Some researchers believe that AGI is achievable in the near future, while others argue that it could take decades or even centuries.

---

[3] [3] Zoe L. (Nov 16, 2022). "General AI vs Narrow AI" https://levity.ai/blog/general-ai-vs-narrow-ai

1.2.3.1.2 Weak artificial intelligence versus strong artificial intelligence

The distinction between weak and strong AI[4] is closely related to the categorization of narrow versus general AI, but focuses on the philosophical implications of AI capabilities.

Weak AI refers to the idea that AI systems can simulate intelligence and perform tasks that appear intelligent but lack true awareness or understanding. This perspective sees AI as a tool for solving specific problems and achieving practical goals, without necessarily replicating the full spectrum of human cognitive abilities. Weak AI systems are designed to mimic intelligent behavior, but lack the underlying consciousness or subjective experience that humans possess. They operate on the basis of algorithms and data, following pre-programmed rules and patterns to achieve specific results.

Strong AI, on the other hand, postulates that AI systems can, in principle, achieve true intelligence and consciousness, equivalent or superior to that of humans. This view suggests that AI could potentially have subjective experiences, emotions and self-awareness. A strong AI would not merely simulate intelligence, but possess true understanding and the ability to experience the world in a way similar to that of humans. However, Strong AI remains a theoretical concept, and there is no consensus among researchers and philosophers as to whether it is achievable or even desirable. The development of Strong AI raises ethical and philosophical questions about the nature of consciousness, the potential risks of super-intelligent machines and the implications for humanity.

[4] [4] Selmer B. (Jul 12, 2018), "Artificial Intelligence", "8. Philosophy of Artificial Intelligence",
https://plato.stanford.edu/entries/artificial-intelligence/#StroVersWeakAI

1.2.4 The main paradigms

1.2.4.1 Symbolic artificial intelligence

Symbolic AI[5] , also known as Good Old-Fashioned AI (GOFAI), is an AI paradigm that dominated the first decades of AI research. It is based on the idea that knowledge can be represented using symbols and manipulated using logical rules. Symbolic AI systems use formal logic and symbolic reasoning to solve problems, make decisions and draw conclusions. This approach has been successful in developing expert systems, which are AI programs that mimic the decision-making ability of human experts in specific fields. These systems rely on a knowledge base of facts and rules, which are used to deduce new knowledge and solve problems through logical deduction. Symbolic AI has been particularly effective in fields with well-defined rules and structured knowledge, such as chess and medical diagnosis. However, it has encountered limitations in uncertainty management, common sense reasoning and learning from data, leading to the emergence of other AI paradigms.

1.2.4.2 Machine learning

Machine learning (ML)[6] , a sub-field of AI that has grown in importance in recent years due to its ability to learn from data and improve performance on tasks without being explicitly programmed. ML algorithms can analyze large datasets, identify patterns and make predictions or decisions based on the learned patterns. This approach has been very successful in a variety of applications, such as image recognition, natural language processing and recommender systems. We'll look at machine learning in more detail later.

ML's relationship with AI in general is that of a powerful tool within a broader framework. While AI encompasses a wide range of techniques and approaches, ML provides a data-driven methodology for achieving AI goals. ML algorithms can

---

[5] [5] Data Camp (May 2023). "What is symbolic AI?". https://www.datacamp.com/blog/what-is-symbolic-ai

[6] [6] Selmer B. (Jul 12, 2018), "Artificial Intelligence", "4.1 Bloom in machine learning". https://plato.stanford.edu/entries/artificial-intelligence/#BlooMachLear

be used to develop intelligent agents capable of learning and adapting to new situations, making them valuable tools for solving complex problems and achieving the ambitious goals of AI. Unlike symbolic AI, which relies on explicit rules and knowledge representation, ML algorithms learn from data via a process of trial and error, adjusting their internal parameters to improve performance over time. This data-driven approach has proved highly effective in dealing with complex, unstructured data, making ML a cornerstone of modern AI research and applications.

1.3 Machine learning

1.3.1 A definition

Machine learning[7] is a complex sub-field of artificial intelligence that focuses on the development of systems capable of learning and making decisions from data. Unlike traditional programming, where tasks are executed according to explicit instructions, machine learning relies on algorithms capable of recognizing patterns, making predictions and improving their performance autonomously as they are exposed to more data. This process involves training models on large data sets, enabling them to make accurate predictions or take intelligent actions without human intervention. Machine learning is the science of enabling computers to act without being explicitly programmed. In essence, machine learning algorithms use historical data as input to predict new output values. It's a method that enables computers to analyze past experience and make data-driven decisions, a process similar to human learning but on a much greater scale and speed.

1.3.2 The story

Machine learning[8] , an essential component of artificial intelligence, is a field that has developed thanks to the convergence of various scientific disciplines. Its history is marked by the quest to endow machines with the ability to learn and

[7] [3] Zoe L. (Nov 16, 2022). "General AI vs Narrow AI" https://levity.ai/blog/general-ai-vs-narrow-ai

[8] [8] Nailman A. (August 24, 2023), "The Evolution of Machine Learning: A Brief History and Timeline." https://machinelearningmodels.org/the-evolution-of-machine-learning-a-brief-history-and-timeline/

improve from experience. The term "machine learning" was first coined in 1959 by Arthur Samuel, who developed a checkers program capable of learning from its games. This marked the beginning of a discipline that would encompass a variety of algorithms and techniques aimed at enabling computers to perform tasks that traditionally required human intelligence.

The development of machine learning has been punctuated by periods of intense optimism, followed by setbacks and renewed efforts. From the early days of perceptrons and symbolic artificial intelligence to recent advances in deep learning, the field has continually pushed back the frontiers of what machines can achieve. Today, machine learning stands as a testament to human ingenuity, transforming industries and shaping the future of technology. We'll now take a look at the main points in the history of machine learning:

1.3.2.1 Origins

The era of the genesis of machine learning, spanning the 1950s and 1960s, represents a seminal chapter in the annals of computer science. It was a period characterized by revolutionary ideas and the first practical implementations of what would become a transformative field. Alan Turing, often hailed as the father of modern computing, laid the philosophical foundations with his thoughts on artificial intelligence and the learning potential of machines. His prescient vision paved the way for Frank Rosenblatt's development of the perceptron in 1957, an early model of a neural network capable of learning and making decisions, embodying the nascent aspirations of machine learning. Arthur Samuel further strengthened the legacy of this era by coining the term "machine learning" in 1959 and demonstrating its potential through his checkers program, which improved performance as he played more games. This era wasn't just about technological innovation; it was about the bold belief that machines could one day emulate the learning abilities of the human mind.

1.3.2.2 The birth

After a period of disillusionment due to the limitations of early artificial intelligence systems, the 1980s marked a renaissance in machine learning, characterized by significant theoretical and practical advances. The decade witnessed the refinement of backpropagation, an algorithm that revolutionized neural networks. This technique, which involves adjusting the weights of connections within the network according to the error rate of the outputs, enabled neural networks to learn from their errors and improve over time. The work of Rumelhart, Hinton and Williams in 1986 was particularly influential, providing a clear demonstration of the potential of backpropagation and rekindling interest in neural networks. This era paved the way for the development of more complex architectures and the deep learning revolution that was to follow.

1.3.2.3 The Ascension of support vector machines

The 1990s marked a pivotal era in the evolution of machine learning, characterized by the rise of Support Vector Machines. Developed at AT&T's Bell Lab by Vladimir Vapnik and colleagues, these systems represented a significant leap forward in the field's ability to classify data. These algorithms excel at finding the optimal hyperplane that separates different classes in a high-dimensional space, which is crucial for tasks such as image recognition and text categorization. The theoretical foundations, rooted in Vapnik-Chervonenkis theory, provided a robust framework for understanding the generalization capabilities of learning machines. This period was not just about algorithmic innovation; it was a time when machine learning began to mature as a discipline, with a growing appreciation of the importance of theory in guiding practical applications.

1.3.2.4 The era of big data

The dawn of the 21st century marked the advent of the Big Data era, a transformative period for machine learning characterized by an unprecedented explosion of data. This era was marked by the digitization of vast quantities of information and the rise of the internet, which collectively generated a deluge of data ready for analysis. Machine learning algorithms, which had gradually grown in sophistication, found a new playground in this data-rich environment. The availability of large data sets enabled the training of more complex models, leading to significant improvements in predictive accuracy and decision-making capabilities. It was during this period that machine learning truly began to flourish, as the synergy between increased computing power and big data provided fertile ground for advances in the field. The Big Data era not only propelled machine learning to new heights, but also laid the foundations for subsequent leaps in AI, such as deep learning and reinforcement learning.

1.3.3 Applications

Nevertheless, following the evolution of machine learning, it has seen a multitude of applications such as predictive analytics, where algorithms predict future events based on historical data. In healthcare, machine learning models identify patterns and aid diagnosis and the development of personalized treatment plans. The financial sector uses it for risk management and algorithmic trading. In retail, machine learning personalizes customer experiences through recommendation systems. It also plays a key role in autonomous vehicles, enabling them to interpret sensory data and make decisions. What's more, machine learning algorithms are integral to the development of natural language processing, which powers virtual assistants and translates languages with remarkable accuracy. Here are some of the applications of machine learning today:

1.3.3.1 Image recognition

Machine learning has revolutionized image recognition, enabling computers to identify and categorize visual content with remarkable accuracy. By training on huge datasets, algorithms can discern complex patterns in pixels, distinguishing between faces, objects and even emotions. This technology underpins diverse applications, from security systems with facial recognition to medical diagnostics that can detect anomalies in imaging scans.

1.3.3.2 Natural language processing

Natural Language Processing enables machines to understand and interact with human language, transforming plain text and speech into meaningful data. It encompasses tasks such as translation, sentiment analysis and chatbot communication. With machine learning, systems can learn the subtleties of language, including idioms and colloquialisms, making interactions more natural and intuitive.

1.3.3.3 Fraud detection s

In the financial sector, machine learning is a powerful tool for identifying fraudulent activity. Algorithms analyze transaction patterns to detect anomalies that may indicate fraud. This proactive approach helps institutions minimize risk and protect their customers from financial threats.

1.3.3.4 Health applications

Machine learning in healthcare is paving the way for personalized medicine and improved diagnostic accuracy. Algorithms can predict patient outcomes, aid treatment planning and even aid drug discovery by analyzing medical records and genetic data.

1.3.3.5 Autonomous vehicles

Integrating machine learning into autonomous vehicles is essential for safe navigation. Algorithms process sensory data to make real-time decisions, enabling vehicles to respond to dynamic road conditions and improve safety for all road users.

1.3.3.6 Recommendation systems

Machine learning powers recommendation systems that curate personalized content for users. By analyzing user behavior and preferences, these systems suggest products, movies or articles, enhancing user experience and engagement on platforms.

1.3.4 Types of automatic learning[9]

1.3.4.1 Supervised learning

Supervised learning is an intellectual pursuit within artificial intelligence. It is distinguished by its use of labeled data sets to train algorithms to classify data or predict results accurately. Imagine a diligent student, the algorithm, learning

[9] [9] Anushka J. (29 Nov 2023), "Types Of Machine Learning". https://www.geeksforgeeks.org/types-of-machine-learning/

from a book full of solved exercises; the labeled data provides the correct answers. As the student encounters new problems, he applies the patterns learned to find solutions, refining his understanding over time. This process reflects the essence of supervised learning, where the algorithm iteratively adjusts its parameters through a method known as cross-validation, searching for a model that fits perfectly. Supervised learning is divided into two types:

1.3.4.1.1 Regression

Regression in machine learning is a statistical technique that models and analyzes relationships between dependent and independent variables. It is used to predict the value of an outcome variable by

function of one or more predictor variables. The aim is to find the best fitting line or curve that minimizes the difference between predicted and actual values. This method is fundamental in forecasting scenarios, such as the prediction of real estate prices or stock market trends, where the result is a continuous quantity.

There are several algorithms that are used for regression in machine learning, including:

- ✓ **Linear regression** , which is a statistical method used to model the relationship between a dependent variable and one or more independent variables. The model assumes that the relationship between the variables is linear, which is expressed by equation :

$$y = \beta_0 + \beta_1 x$$

Where (y) is the dependent variable, (x) is the independent variable, (beta_0) is the y-intercept, and (beta_1) is the slope of the line. This method is widely used in various scientific fields for predictive modeling and data analysis. It is particularly useful when the aim is to understand the impact of one variable on another and make predictions based on this relationship.

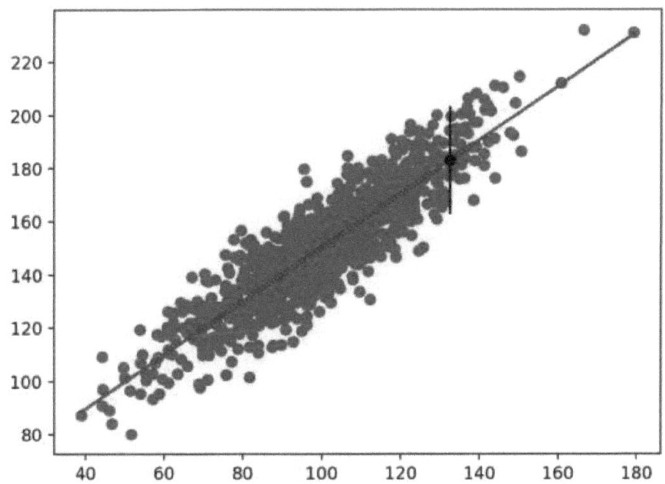

Figure 1Diagram of a linear function

1.3.4.1.2 Classification

Classification in machine learning is a supervised learning technique where an algorithm is trained to categorize new data points into predefined classes. It's a process of discernment, similar to a teacher grading essays, where each piece of data, like a student's work, is evaluated and labeled according to

learned features. This method is essential in applications ranging from e-mail filtering to medical diagnosis, where the ability to accurately assign categories to data can lead to meaningful insights and actions. Classification also has several algorithms at its disposal, one of the best known being :

✓ **Logistic regression** , which is a statistical model in supervised machine learning that predicts the probability of a binary outcome. It is used when the dependent variable is categorical and can take two possible outcomes, such as "yes" or "no", "success" or "failure". The logistic function, also known as the sigmoid function, maps any real number into a value between 0 and 1, which can be interpreted as a probability. The model is defined by the logistic function :

$$\sigma(x) = \frac{1}{1 + e^{-x_1}}$$

Where (x) is the linear combination of independent variables. The model coefficients are estimated using maximum likelihood estimation, which seeks to find the parameter values that make the observed results most likely.

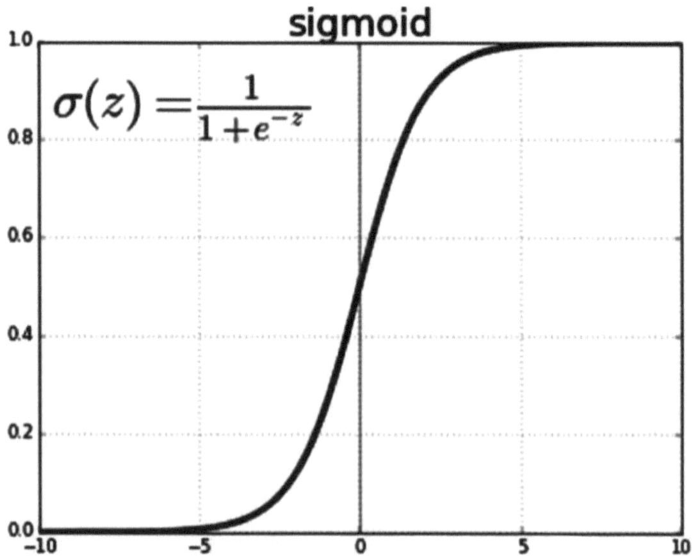

Figure 2Diagram of a sigmoid function

However, there are many machine learning models that can be used for both regression and classification, including :

- ✓ **Decision trees :** Decision trees in machine learning embody the decision-making process through a tree model of choices. Each internal node represents a "decision" based on an attribute, each branch indicates the result of this decision and each leaf node signifies the final prediction or classification. Mathematically, the purity of a node, which influences the decision at each branch, is often calculated using metrics such as Gini impurity or entropy. For example, Gini impurity is given by :

$$IG(p) = 1 - \sum p_i^2$$

where (p_i) is the probability of an element being in class (i) in a set (J).

✓ **Random forests :** Random forests in machine learning are an ensemble learning method that works by constructing a multitude of decision trees during training and outputting the class, which is the mode of the classes (classification) or the average prediction (regression) of the individual trees. Mathematically, a random forest is designed to mitigate the large variance of a single decision tree. If (T_b(x)) is the prediction of the ($b^{\text{ème}}$) tree, then the prediction of the random forest (y) for an input (x) is given by:

$$y = \frac{1}{B} \sum T_b(x)$$

Where (B) is the number of trees. The link between random forests and decision trees is fundamental; random forests build on the simplicity of decision trees by creating a 'forest' of them, thus improving robustness and accuracy.

1.3.4.2 Unsupervised learning

Unsupervised learning is a subset of machine learning algorithms that operate on directionless, unlabeled data. It aims to model the underlying structure or distribution in the data in order to learn more about the data. It is used for clustering and association problems where the task is to discover inherent groupings in the data, identify representations, correlations or patterns among features without the influence of an outcome variable. This form of learning is essential for exploratory data analysis, hidden pattern identification or feature learning. There are two broad categories of use for unsupervised learning:

Clustering in machine learning is an unsupervised learning technique that groups a set of objects in such a way that objects in the same group, called a cluster, are more similar to each other than to objects in other groups. It's a method that doesn't rely on predefined labels or results, but rather seeks to discover the intrinsic structure within the data. Clustering algorithms evaluate data characteristics to identify natural groupings, often using similarity or distance measures, such as Euclidean distance or cosine similarity, to determine the proximity of data points. This technique is essential in a variety of fields, including market segmentation, social network analysis and biological data analysis, where it helps to discover patterns and organize information. There are several clustering algorithms, one of the most popular being :

1.3.4.2.1 K-means clustering

K-means clustering is an unsupervised learning algorithm that partitions a dataset into K distinct, non-overlapping subsets, or clusters.

The aim is to minimize the variance within each cluster. The process begins by selecting K initial centroids, one for each cluster. The algorithm then assigns each data point to the nearest centroid, and recalculates the centroids as the average of all points in the cluster. This iterative process continues until the centroids stabilize, and the clusters are as homogeneous as possible within themselves and as distinct as possible from each other.

1.3.4.2.2 Dimensionality reduction

Dimensionality reduction is a transformation process that simplifies the complexity of high-dimensional data. It's a strategic condensation, where algorithms streamline vast arrays of features into a manageable essence, rather like an expert cartographer distilling a map of the world into a concise city guide. This technique, essential for combating the 'scourge of dimensionality', improves model performance by filtering out noise and redundancy, sharpening the focus on the most informative attributes. It is implemented by methods such as :

- ✓ **Principal Component Analysis :** which is a statistical procedure in machine learning that transforms a complex dataset with many variables into a simplified structure. It achieves this by identifying new axes, called principal components, which are orthogonal to each other and capture the maximum variance in the data. The essence of PCA is to reduce dimensionality while retaining as much information as possible. Mathematically, if we have a data set with variables :

(X_1, X_2, ..., X_n), PCA seeks to find a set of (p) principal components (Y_1, Y_2, ..., Y_p) where (p < n), such that :

$$Y_i = a_1X_1 + a_2X_2 + \cdots + a_nX_n$$

1.3.4.3 Other types

Having looked at the fields of supervised and unsupervised learning, we will now turn to exploring other types of machine learning models. These models broaden the horizons of our understanding and application of artificial intelligence, offering new perspectives and methodologies for tackling complex problems starting with reinforcement learning :

1.3.4.3.1 Reinforcement learning[10]

Reinforcement learning is a paradigm within machine learning where an agent learns to make decisions by interacting with an environment. Unlike deep learning, which relies on large data sets and neural networks to recognize patterns, reinforcement learning works through a system of rewards and penalties. It is a dynamic process in which the agent learns optimal behaviors through trial and error, aiming to maximize a cumulative reward over time. This approach is particularly effective in sequential decision-making tasks and complex environments where the right action to take is not immediately obvious. Reinforcement learning uses several concepts such as :

[10] [10] Robert J. (Jul 31, 2023), "Reinforcement learning: definition and application". https://datascientest.com/reinforcement-learning

➢ **Dynamic programming :** which is a methodological framework that simplifies complex decision-making processes by breaking them down into simpler, more manageable sub-problems. It is a form of mathematical optimization that uses the concept of the Bellman equation to find optimal policies. Dynamic programming is particularly effective in scenarios where problems have overlapping sub-problems and an optimal substructure, making it a powerful tool for solving Markov Decision Processes. As a subcategory of reinforcement learning, dynamic programming provides the theoretical foundations for algorithms that learn to make sequences of decisions maximizing cumulative reward. It is the structured, recursive approach of dynamic programming that informs and enhances the field of reinforcement learning, offering a systematic way of approaching and solving sequential decision problems.

➢ **The Monte Carlo method :** is a computational algorithm that uses repeated random sampling to approximate numerical results. It is a technique that harnesses the power of chance to solve problems that may appear deterministic in principle. In the context of reinforcement learning, Monte Carlo methods are used to estimate value functions based on experience, without requiring a model of the environment's dynamics. This approach is particularly useful for problems where the environment is unknown or too complex to model explicitly.

1.3.4.3.2 Deep learning

Deep learning[11] is a sophisticated branch of machine learning that uses multi-layer neural networks to mimic the complex processing capabilities of the human brain. It's a considerable leap beyond traditional machine learning, exploiting the depth of neural networks to discern patterns and make decisions from vast quantities of data. The term 'deep' in deep learning refers to the number of layers through which data is transformed. The more layers there are, the more complex the representations and abstractions of the data can be, making deep learning

---

[11] [11] Ngaleu A. K. (Jul 4, 2022), "Deep Learning: Definition, concepts and examples". https://datascientest.com/reinforcement-learning

particularly apt for tasks such as image and speech recognition. The correlation between deep learning and neural networks is intrinsic, as the latter form the architecture that deep learning algorithms use to learn and make intelligent decisions. Neural networks, on the other hand, are computational architectures inspired by the biological neural networks of the human brain. These networks are made up of layers of interconnected nodes, or neurons, which process input data through a series of transformations and connections. Each neuron applies a set of weights to its inputs, which are then adjusted during the learning process to optimize network performance. The fundamental operation of a neural network involves the summation of weighted inputs and the application of a non-linear activation function, facilitating complex pattern recognition and decision-making tasks.

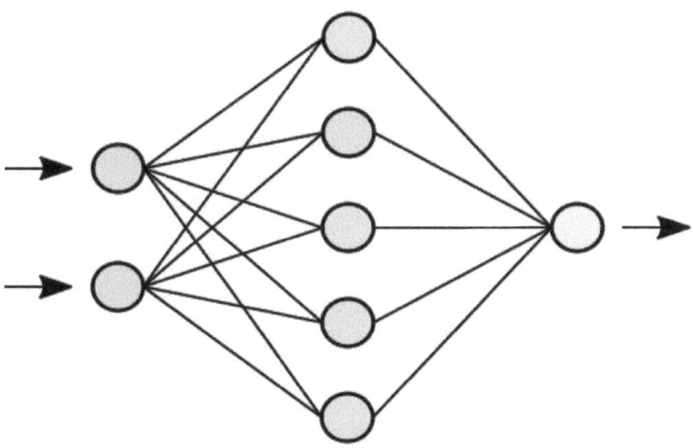

Figure 3Basic diagram of a neural network

There are many mathematical concepts involved in building a neural network[12], such as :

➤ **Nodes and layers, weights and biases :** In neural network architecture, nodes and layers form the structural basis. Nodes, similar to the neurons in the

[12] [12] Google, (Jul 31, 2023), "Neural Networks: Structure". https://developers.google.com/machine-learning/crash-course/introduction-to-neural-networks/anatomy

human brain, are the basic computing units that process and transmit information. They are organized into layers: input, hidden and output. The nodes in each layer receive inputs, perform calculations and transmit the output to the next layer. The mathematics behind this involves transforming the input data through a series of operations defined by the network structure.

Weights are the parameters that determine the strength of the connection between nodes. They multiply the input data, enabling the network to learn complex patterns by adjusting these weights during the learning process. The mathematical representation of this operation for a single node can be expressed as a weighted sum of its inputs:

$$\textbf{sortie} = \sum(\textbf{entrée} \times \textbf{poids})$$

Biases are additional parameters that shift the activation function, ensuring that even when all inputs are zero, the neuron can still activate if the bias is set correctly. The bias allows the model to better adapt to the data, providing the flexibility needed for accurate predictions. The equation for the output of a node, including the bias, is :

$$\textbf{sortie} = \sum(\textbf{entrée} \times \textbf{poids}) + \textbf{biais}$$

- **Loss functions :** In neural networks, loss functions are the mathematical compasses that guide the learning process. They quantify the difference between the results predicted by the network and the actual target values. The essence of a loss function is to provide a measure of error that the network aims to minimize during training.

- **Activation functions :** In neural networks, activation functions are the mathematical gatekeepers that determine a neuron's output. They are crucial for introducing non-linearity into the network, enabling it to learn and model complex relationships. The function takes the weighted sum of inputs and bias as its argument and transforms it into an output, which is then passed on to the next layer. This transformation is essential as it enables the network to perform operations beyond simple linear operations, making tasks such as image and speech recognition possible. Common activation functions include the sigmoid (the same function used in logistic regression discussed earlier), which squashes values between 0 and 1, and the ReLU, which only lets positive values through.

1.4 Conclusion

In conclusion, this chapter has offered a comprehensive overview of the fundamental concepts, paradigms and techniques of artificial intelligence and machine learning, laying the essential foundations for understanding these constantly evolving fields.

We began by exploring the definition and history of artificial intelligence and machine learning, tracing their evolution from the early days of symbolic AI to the current era of deep neural networks. This historical perspective gave us a better understanding of the foundations on which modern AI technologies are based.

Next, we took an in-depth look at the different types of machine learning, focusing on supervised, unsupervised and reinforcement learning. This analysis highlighted the diversity of approaches available to AI researchers and practitioners, each with its own strengths and specific applications.

Finally, our exploration of machine learning algorithms and techniques highlighted the crucial importance of mathematics and statistics in this field. From regression and classification methods to clustering and dimensionality reduction techniques, neural networks and deep learning, we saw how these tools enable AI systems to analyze complex data and make intelligent decisions.

Ultimately, this chapter has highlighted the multifaceted and dynamic nature of artificial intelligence and machine learning. It has underlined the importance for professionals and researchers to master not only the fundamental concepts, but also the ever-evolving algorithms and techniques that shape these fields. By embracing this knowledge and staying at the forefront of innovation, we can truly harness the power of AI to solve complex problems and transform various aspects of our society and economy.

DIGITAL MARKETING: HISTORY, DEFINITIONS AND TYPOLOGY

CHAPTER II :

► DIGITAL MAQRKETING: HISTORY, DEFINITIONS AND TYPOLOGY

2.1 Introduction

In this chapter, we'll explore the essential foundations of digital marketing, starting with an in-depth definition of the concept and an overview of its historical development. Digital marketing, which encompasses a variety of strategies such as inbound marketing, search engine optimization, email marketing and online advertising, has transformed the way companies interact with their target audience in the digital age.

We then take a detailed look at the different types of digital marketing, focusing on inbound and outbound approaches. We'll analyze their distinctive features, advantages and disadvantages, as well as their specific applications in various business contexts.

After laying these conceptual foundations, we'll look at the essential tools, platforms and channels of digital marketing. We'll explore a range of data analysis and social media management tools, such as Google Analytics and Hootsuite, that enable marketers to measure and optimize their efforts. We'll also look at online advertising platforms such as Google Ads and major social networks, as well as email marketing and content creation tools that are crucial to an effective digital marketing strategy.

This chapter aims to provide a comprehensive understanding of the key concepts, strategies and tools of digital marketing, laying the foundations for further exploration of their practical application in the modern business landscape.

2.2 Digital marketing

2.2.1 key concepts

2.2.1.1 A definition

Digital marketing[13] is the art and science of interacting with a global audience in the digital space. It's about creating compelling stories and experiences that resonate on a personal level, using the vast interconnected network of the Internet. This innovative approach to marketing harnesses digital technologies to reach and engage consumers in a more targeted and interactive way than ever before. At the heart of digital marketing is connecting with people where they spend a significant part of their time: online. This ubiquitous online presence offers brands an unprecedented opportunity to interact with their target audience on an ongoing, personalized basis.

It's a discipline that combines creativity and data-driven strategies to understand and respond to consumer needs, fostering meaningful interactions that build trust and community. This two-way approach enables brands not only to communicate their message, but also to listen and respond to consumer feedback in real time, creating a dynamic and evolving dialogue. Digital marketing is a composite field, segmented into various strategies such as search engine optimization (SEO), content marketing, social media marketing, e-mail marketing, mobile marketing and so on. Each of these strategies plays a crucial role in the overall digital ecosystem, offering unique ways of reaching and engaging consumers at different stages of their buying journey.

Each strategy serves a specific purpose in the digital marketing ecosystem, aiming to optimize a brand's online presence, interact with the target audience and generate conversions. For example, SEO helps increase a brand's visibility in organic search results, while content marketing aims to attract and hold consumers' attention with valuable, relevant information. Social media marketing exploits the viral and interactive nature of social platforms to create

---

[13] [13] Novak j. (Feb 16, 2024), "What is digital marketing? Types, Strategies, & Best Practices". https://www.forbes.com/advisor/business/what-is-digital-marketing/

brand engagement and recognition, while e-mail marketing offers direct, personalized communication with consumers. These strategies are interconnected, forming a coherent framework that supports a brand's overall digital marketplace, creating a seamless, integrated user experience across diverse digital touchpoints.

2.2.1.2 The story

Digital marketing began its journey in the 1980s, a decade that saw the convergence of data storage capabilities and marketing ambitions. This period marked a crucial turning point in the evolution of marketing, from traditional methods to a more data-driven, technology-driven approach. With the proliferation of personal computers, marketers acquired the ability to systematically store and analyze customer information, giving birth to database marketing. This innovation has enabled companies to collect, organize and exploit vast quantities of consumer data, paving the way for more targeted and personalized marketing strategies.

It was the forerunner of the digital marketing we know today, enabling more personalized and targeted marketing strategies, capable of adapting to consumer behaviors and preferences. This ability to segment audiences and tailor messages to specific consumer characteristics laid the foundations for a more effective, customer-centric marketing approach. The 1980s laid the foundations for the digital marketing revolution, paving the way for the rapid evolution of online marketing techniques over the decades that followed. This period saw the emergence of fundamental concepts such as customer relationship management (CRM) and data-driven market segmentation, which have become mainstays of modern digital marketing.

Despite seminal developments in the 1980s, the term "digital marketing" was really coined in the 1990s. This decade was marked by the advent of the Web 1.0 platform, which enabled users to find information but not yet to interact with it directly. This first iteration of the World Wide Web laid the foundations for the digital revolution to come, offering companies a new platform to present their products and services to a global audience. The 1990s saw the Internet become commercialized, and with it the first clickable banner went online, heralding the beginning of the digital advertising space as we know it. This innovation marked a turning point in the history of marketing, introducing the concept of interactive advertising that could be measured in real time.

This clickable banner was published by AT&T[14] , a telecommunications giant, on October 27, 1994. It is shown in the figure below:

Figure 4The first clickable advertising banner on the Internet

This banner ad, although simple by today's standards, marked the beginning of a new era in digital marketing. It introduced the concept of interactive advertising on the Internet, enabling users to click directly on an ad to obtain more information or make a purchase. This innovation paved the way for new forms of advertising measurement and engagement, laying the foundations for today's complex digital advertising ecosystem.

However, digital marketing really took off in the 2000s with the bursting of the Internet bubble, a period of intense speculation and investment in Internet-based businesses. This era, despite its tumultuous end, played a crucial role in the evolution of digital marketing. The bursting of the bubble led to a re-evaluation of online business models and an increased focus on measurable, profitable marketing strategies. This period saw the emergence of new technologies and platforms that redefined the way companies interacted with their customers online.

This era, despite its tumultuous end, paved the way for the rapid development of digital marketing, as companies began to recognize the potential of the Internet as a marketing platform. Lessons learned from the bursting of the bubble led to a

[14] [14] Chantrel F. (Oct 28, 2019), "the first banner ad celebrates 25 years".
https://www.blogdumoderateur.com/premiere-banniere-pub/

more strategic and analytical approach to digital marketing, with an increased focus on return on investment (ROI) and campaign measurability. The emergence of social media platforms has further catalyzed this growth, offering new avenues for brands to engage consumers and personalize their marketing efforts. Platforms like Facebook, LinkedIn and Twitter have transformed the way brands communicate with their audiences, enabling more direct and personal interactions on a massive scale.

Later, the digital marketing landscape was further consolidated by the emergence of cell phones. This technological leap brought digital marketing into the hands of consumers, making mobile marketing the norm. The advent of smartphones, in particular, revolutionized the way consumers accessed information and interacted with brands. This evolution necessitated the rapid adaptation of digital marketing strategies to meet the needs of a public constantly connected and on the move.

The ubiquity of smartphones has transformed the way brands interact with consumers, underlining the need for mobile-optimized content and advertising strategies tailored to an active lifestyle. This transformation has led to the emergence of new forms of digital marketing, such as location-based marketing, branded mobile apps, and in-app advertising. Marketers have had to rethink their approaches to creating seamless, consistent experiences across all devices, recognizing that consumers now move effortlessly from desktop to mobile throughout their buying journey.

2.2.2 The types[15]

2.2.2.1 Inbound digital marketing

Inbound marketing is a contemporary marketing methodology that focuses on attracting customers through relevant and useful content and interactions. This approach represents a paradigm shift from traditional marketing methods, focusing on creating value for consumers rather than interrupting their

---

[15] [15] Chris A. (Feb 25, 2024), "12 Types Of Digital Marketing [And How They Work]." https://www.reliablesoft.net/types-of-digital-marketing/

experience. It differs from outbound marketing, which involves contacting potential customers regardless of their interest or readiness. Inbound marketing recognizes that modern consumers are more informed and skeptical of traditional marketing messages, and therefore seeks to build relationships based on trust and added value.

Inbound marketing strategies focus on creating quality content that matches the interests and needs of a target audience, drawing them to a company's offerings. This approach involves a thorough understanding of the customer journey, pain points and information needs at each stage of that journey. By providing relevant and useful content, companies can position themselves as valuable resources and thought leaders in their field, naturally attracting qualified prospects to their products or services. Inbound marketing can be broken down into several types:

2.2.2.1.1 Search engine optimization marketing

SEO marketing, or search engine optimization, is a strategic process aimed at improving the visibility and ranking of a website or web page in organic search engine results. This complex discipline combines technical, creative and analytical elements to improve a site's relevance and authority in the eyes of search engines. It involves a variety of techniques such as keyword optimization, the creation of high-quality content, link building and ensuring that the website is mobile-friendly and has fast loading times.

Keyword optimization involves the research and strategic integration of relevant terms that the target audience uses to search for information related to the company or industry. High-quality content creation goes beyond simply including keywords; it involves producing informative, engaging and useful content that addresses users' needs and questions. Link building involves obtaining inbound links from high-quality, relevant websites, which reinforces the site's authority in the eyes of search engines.

The aim is to align website content with the intent of potential visitors, making the site more likely to be found by users looking for related information or services. By improving visibility in organic search results, SEO can lead to increased qualified traffic to the website, improved brand recognition and, ultimately, higher conversions and sales.

2.2.2.1.2 E-mail marketing

E-mail marketing is a nuanced approach to contacting potential customers with opt-in e-mail communications. This strategy relies on building and maintaining a list of engaged subscribers who have expressly chosen to receive communications from the brand. It's a permission-based strategy that respects the user's choice and interest in the brand, which distinguishes it from spam or unsolicited communications.

By sending relevant and valuable content to individuals who have explicitly chosen to receive it, companies can cultivate these hot prospects, guiding them through the buyer's journey with personalized messages. This approach enables direct, personalized communication with the target audience, offering opportunities for segmentation and personalization based on subscribers' behaviors, preferences and past interactions.

E-mail marketing can take many forms, such as regular newsletters, promotional campaigns, automated e-mail sequences for customer onboarding, or transactional e-mails linked to specific purchases or interactions. Effective e-mail marketing relies on the creation of valuable content, precise segmentation of the subscriber list, appropriate timing of mailings, and ongoing optimization based on the analysis of performance metrics such as open rates, click-through rates and conversion rates.

2.2.2.1.3 Influence marketing

Influencer marketing is a strategy that involves working with people with a strong presence on social networks to promote products, services or campaigns. This approach capitalizes on the trust and credibility these influencers have established with their audience, offering brands a way to reach and engage target audiences in a more authentic and relational way.

These influencers have the power to influence the purchasing decisions of others due to their authority, knowledge, position or relationship with their audience.

They can vary in audience size, from micro-influencers with smaller but highly engaged followings, to macro-influencers and celebrities with millions of subscribers. Each type of influencer can offer unique advantages depending on campaign objectives and target audience.

Brands partner with influencers to harness the trust of their followers and extend their reach within specific target markets. This collaboration can take various forms, such as sponsored publications, product demonstrations, contests, or even long-term collaborations where the influencer becomes a brand ambassador. The effectiveness of influencer marketing lies in the authenticity of the collaboration, the alignment between influencer, brand and audience, and the creation of engaging and relevant content that resonates with the target audience.

2.2.2.1.4 Blog marketing

Blog marketing is an aspect of content marketing that uses blogs as a means of communicating and interacting with a target audience. This dynamic approach enables companies, individuals or entities to create and maintain a lasting and engaging online presence. It's a dynamic approach where companies, individuals or entities create and maintain a blog to publish content relevant to their industry or interests.

This content can range from informative articles, thought leadership pieces, to product or service updates. Blogs offer a flexible platform for sharing in-depth information, industry analysis, practical advice, and brand stories. They can cover a wide range of formats, including text, images, infographics, and even embedded videos, enabling a multimedia approach to brand storytelling.

The aim is to attract readers who can become customers, establishing the blog as a credible source of information and a hub of community engagement. By regularly providing valuable content, companies can position their blog as a go-to resource in their field, attracting organic traffic via search engines and building a loyal audience. Blog marketing also plays a crucial role in improving a website's SEO, by providing fresh, relevant content that search engines appreciate.

In addition, blogs offer an opportunity for direct engagement with the audience through comments and shares on social networks, helping to build a community around the brand. They also serve as a platform for establishing a brand's authority and expertise in its field, reinforcing trust and credibility with potential customers.

All in all, these elements represent the essence of inbound marketing, with its distinct advantages and disadvantages. Among the benefits, inbound marketing is recognized for its cost-effectiveness, often requiring less financial investment than traditional marketing methods. This approach focuses on the creation of valuable content and the optimization of existing digital channels, rather than on the purchase of costly advertising space or the implementation of large-scale advertising campaigns.

It also excels at generating high-quality leads that are more likely to convert into customers due to the targeted nature of the content. By attracting prospects who are actively seeking information or solutions in the company's field, inbound marketing tends to generate more qualified and engaged leads. These prospects are often further along in their buying journey, and therefore more likely to convert.

What's more, inbound marketing fosters long-term relationships with customers by providing ongoing, valuable information and interacting with them on a variety of platforms. This customer-centric approach helps build trust and loyalty, transforming customers into brand ambassadors. By consistently delivering value through informative content and meaningful interactions, companies can cultivate a loyal customer base who are more likely to make repeat purchases and recommend the brand to others.

2.2.2.2 Outbound marketing

Outbound marketing is a proactive approach in which companies take the initiative to contact potential customers through a variety of channels. This traditional form of marketing involves "pushing" marketing messages to a wide audience, regardless of their initial interest or receptivity. This form of marketing is characterized by its direct and sometimes intrusive nature, as it seeks to broadcast messages to a wide audience, often without precise targeting.

Outbound marketing includes several types, such as :

2.2.2.2.1 Display ads

Display ads are a form of digital advertising that visually convey a commercial message using text, logos, animations, videos, photographs or other graphics. These ads are ubiquitous on the Internet, appearing on various websites, mobile applications and social media platforms. They are designed to grab users' attention and entice them to click to find out more about the advertised product or service.

Display advertisers often target users with particular characteristics to increase ad effectiveness. This targeting can be based on demographic, geographic, behavioral or contextual factors. For example, an ad may be served to users in a certain age bracket, living in a specific geographic area, or who have recently searched for similar products.

These ads are strategically placed on various websites and platforms to capture the attention of potential customers and encourage them to interact with the brand, whether to make a purchase, find out more about a product or simply remember the brand for future reference. Locations can include banners at the top of web pages, inserts in content, sidebar ads, or even full-screen (interstitial) ads.

Display ads are renowned for their ability to enhance brand visibility and can be tailored to the context of the site or the interests of the viewer, making them a versatile tool in a marketer's arsenal. They can be used for a variety of marketing purposes, such as raising brand awareness, generating leads, or promoting specific products. What's more, retargeting technologies enable advertisers to show display ads to users who have already interacted with their website, thus increasing the chances of conversion.

2.2.2.2.2 E-mail spamming

E-mail spamming, commonly known as spam, is the practice of sending unsolicited messages, usually of a commercial nature, en masse to an indistinct set of recipients. This form of advertising is often perceived as intrusive and unwanted, clogging up inboxes with messages that recipients haven't requested and are generally of no interest to them.

Spam can take many forms, from unsolicited promotional offers to scams and phishing attempts. Spammers often use automated techniques to collect e-mail addresses and send messages en masse, making the practice inexpensive but potentially very disruptive for recipients.

The term 'spam' itself has become synonymous with unwanted electronic communication, reflecting widespread frustration with this invasive marketing tactic. The origin of the term 'spam' in this context can be traced back to a Monty Python sketch, in which the word 'spam' was repeated excessively and annoyingly, reflecting the repetitive and annoying nature of unsolicited e-mails.

Despite its bad reputation, e-mail spamming persists because of its low cost and the ease with which advertisers can reach a vast audience. However, it's important to note that the practice is illegal in many countries and goes against digital marketing best practice.

2.2.2.2.3 Advertising on social networks

Paid advertising on social networks is a digital marketing strategy that involves distributing sponsored content on social media platforms to reach a wider audience. This form of advertising enables companies to precisely target their audience based on various demographic, behavioral and interest criteria, offering a level of personalization and precision unmatched by traditional forms of advertising.

These ads can take a variety of forms, such as images, videos, carousels, and more, each designed to engage users and prompt them to take action. Formats vary by platform, but can include News Feed ads, sponsored stories, video ads, or even more interactive formats like polls or games.

2.2.2.2.4 Search engine advertising marketing

Search engine advertising marketing, also known as pay-per-click or search engine marketing, is an Internet marketing model in which advertisers pay a fee every time one of their ads is clicked. In essence, it's a way of buying visits to sites, rather than trying to get those visits organically.

It allows advertisers to bid for the placement of ads in a search engine's sponsored links when someone performs a search on a keyword related to their commercial offer. These ads generally appear at the top of the search results, above the organic results, or in the side column.

PPC offers several key advantages:

- ✓ Precise targeting: Advertisers can target users based on their specific search queries, indicating clear intent and interest in a particular product or service.
- ✓ Budget control: Advertisers can set a daily or monthly budget and only pay when a user clicks on their ad.
- ✓ Measurability: PPC campaigns offer detailed performance data, enabling advertisers to continually optimize their campaigns.
- ✓ Speed: Unlike SEO, which can take time to produce results, PPC can generate traffic immediately after launching a campaign.

2.3 Digital marketing, its platforms and channels[16]

2.3.1 Online advertising

Online advertising encompasses a wide range of advertising formats, including banner ads, video ads, social network ads and search engine ads. This form of digital marketing has revolutionized the way companies reach and engage their target audiences, offering unprecedented possibilities for targeting, personalization and measurement.

[16] [16] Ryan D.,Russ H. (July 31, 2023), "Digital Marketing For Dummies", 2nd edition, page 263.

These ads can be targeted according to demographics, interests, behavior and other criteria, enabling companies to reach their target audience precisely and effectively. Targeting can be based on factors such as age, gender, geographic location, stated interests, browsing behavior, purchase history, and much more. This granular targeting capability enables advertisers to create highly relevant messages for specific audience segments, increasing the effectiveness of their campaigns.

Online advertising offers robust measurement and tracking options, enabling marketers to assess the performance of their campaigns and optimize their advertising spend. Advertisers can track metrics such as impressions, clicks, conversion rates, return on investment (ROI), and many other performance indicators. This wealth of data enables continuous campaign optimization, allowing advertisers to adjust their strategies in real time to maximize the effectiveness of their advertising investments.

2.3.1.1 Google Ads

This advertising platform enables companies to create ads that appear in Google search results, as well as on other partner websites in the Google Display Network. Google Ads is one of the most powerful and widely used online advertising platforms, offering unrivalled reach and sophisticated targeting options.

Advertisers can choose from different ad formats, such as text ads, responsive ads, illustrated ads and video ads. Each format has its own advantages and can be used to achieve different marketing objectives. For example, text ads are effective for capturing search intent, while video ads can be more engaging for brand awareness.

Google Ads also offers advanced targeting options, including keyword targeting, demographic targeting, interest-based targeting and retargeting. Keyword targeting enables advertisers to show their ads to users searching for specific terms related to their business. Demographic and interest-based targeting enable specific audiences to be reached based on their characteristics and online behaviors. Retargeting enables advertisers to show ads to users who have already interacted with their website or app, increasing the chances of conversion.

2.3.1.2 Bing Ads

Similar to Google Ads, Bing Ads enables companies to run ads on the Bing search engine and on other partner sites in the Microsoft Audience Network. Although Bing has a smaller market share than Google, it can be a cost-effective advertising channel for some businesses, particularly those targeting specific demographics who are more likely to use Bing.

Bing Ads offers several unique advantages:

✓ Potentially lower cost: Due to lower competition from Google Ads, costs per click (CPC) can be lower on Bing Ads.

✓ Different demographics: Bing tends to attract a slightly older, more affluent audience, which can be advantageous for some companies.

✓ Integration with LinkedIn: Bing Ads enables targeting based on LinkedIn professional profiles, which can be particularly useful for B2B marketing.

✓ Less saturation: With fewer advertisers on the platform, it can be easier to stand out on Bing Ads.

2.3.1.3 Native advertising

Native advertising is an advertising format that integrates seamlessly with the surrounding content, offering a less intrusive advertising experience for users. These ads are designed to look and behave like the natural editorial content of the platform on which they appear, which can increase engagement and reduce the "banner blindness" often associated with traditional advertising formats.

Native ads can appear as sponsored articles, recommended publications or embedded content in users' news feeds. They are particularly effective on social media platforms and publisher sites, where they can blend naturally into the flow of content that users consume.

Benefits of native advertising :

- ✓ Better engagement: Native ads tend to have higher engagement rates than traditional ads.
- ✓ Less intrusive: They offer a better user experience by not disrupting the content flow.
- ✓ Bypassing banner blindness: Users are more likely to pay attention to native ads than to traditional banners.
- ✓ Added value: When well executed, native ads can deliver content that is genuinely useful or interesting to the user.

2.3.1.4 Video advertising

Video advertising is becoming increasingly popular, as it enables companies to tell more engaging stories and present their products or services in a more dynamic way. Video offers a unique opportunity to combine visual and auditory elements to create a stronger emotional impact and convey complex messages more effectively.

- Video platforms such as YouTube and social networks offer a variety of video advertising options, including InStream ads, bumper ads and TrueView ads.
- InStream ads: These ads appear before, during or after the main video content. They can be skippable (allowing users to skip them after a few seconds) or non-ignorable.
- Bumper ads: These are short, 6-second video ads that can't be ignored, ideal for conveying a brief, memorable message.
- TrueView ads: These ads allow viewers to choose which ads they want to watch and when. They are often used for longer, more engaging content.

Social media platforms such as Facebook, Instagram, Twitter, LinkedIn, Pinterest, TikTok and YouTube have become indispensable digital marketing channels. They offer companies a powerful way to interact with their target audience, share content, create communities and promote their products or services. Social media enable two-way communication, where companies can not only broadcast messages, but also listen and respond to their customers' comments and concerns.

2.3.1.5 Facebook

With its vast user base, Facebook offers companies the opportunity to target specific audiences based on their demographics, interests and behaviors. This platform has an impressive amount of data on its users, enabling extremely precise targeting.

Companies can create professional pages, publish updates, share photos and videos, and interact with their fans. These pages serve as virtual showcases for brands, enabling them to build an engaged community around their product or service.

Facebook ads enable precise targeting and offer a variety of format options, including images, videos, carousels and collection ads. Facebook ad formats are constantly evolving, offering new and creative ways to reach and engage target audiences.

2.3.1.6 Instagram

This visual platform is ideal for brands that want to showcase their products or services in an aesthetically pleasing way. Instagram is particularly effective for industries where the visual aspect is paramount, such as fashion, beauty, travel, food, and design.

Businesses can share high-quality photos and videos, use stories to share ephemeral content, and interact with their followers through comments and direct messages. Instagram stories offer a unique opportunity to share more spontaneous and authentic content, strengthening the connection with the audience.

Instagram ads can be seamlessly integrated into users' News Feed, offering a non-intrusive advertising experience. Formats include photo, video, carousel, and stories ads, allowing for great creative flexibility.

2.3.1.7 Twitter

Twitter is a microblogging platform that enables businesses to share rapid updates, industry news and interact with their audience in real time. The real-time nature of Twitter makes it a powerful tool for news and event marketing.

Hashtags play an important role on Twitter, enabling companies to participate in relevant conversations and reach a wider audience. Brands can create their own hashtags for specific campaigns, or participate in existing conversations to increase their visibility.

Twitter ads can be targeted according to users' interests, keywords and behaviors. Ad formats include promoted tweets, promoted accounts and promoted trends, offering various options for reaching and engaging the target audience.

2.3.1.8 LinkedIn

This professional platform is ideal for B2B marketing, enabling companies to connect with other professionals, share industry-relevant content, and promote their products or services to a professional audience. LinkedIn offers a unique environment where users are in a professional frame of mind, which can be particularly beneficial for certain types of business.

LinkedIn Groups provide a space for discussion and networking, enabling companies to establish themselves as thought leaders in their field. These groups can be used to share knowledge, answer questions and build relationships with potential prospects.

LinkedIn ads enable precise targeting based on industry, position and other professional criteria. Advertising options include sponsored ads, sponsored InMail messages and text ads, offering a variety of ways to reach the professional target audience.

2.3.1.9 Pinterest

This visual platform is all about discovery and inspiration, making it a powerful tool for brands selling products or services related to lifestyle, fashion, home decor, food and more. Pinterest is particularly effective at reaching users at the beginning of their buying journey, when they're looking for inspiration and ideas.

Companies can create pinboards to showcase their products, share ideas and inspire users. These boards can be organized by theme, collection or season, providing an attractive visual showcase for a brand's products or services.

Pinterest ads can be targeted based on users' interests, keywords and behaviors. Ad formats include promoted pins, carousel pins and collection pins, allowing brands to showcase their products in creative and engaging ways.

2.3.1.10 TikTok

This short video platform has become incredibly popular with the younger generation. TikTok offers a unique opportunity for brands to show a lighter, more creative side, engaging with their audience in a fun, authentic way.

Companies can create creative and engaging videos to promote their products or services, participate in viral challenges, and collaborate with TikTok influencers. The viral nature of content on TikTok can enable brands to reach a large audience very quickly if their content resonates with users.

TikTok ads can be natively integrated into users' News Feed, offering an immersive advertising experience. Ad formats include In-Feed Ads, Brand Takeovers and Hashtag Challenges, offering a variety of ways to engage the TikTok audience.

2.3.2 Other digital marketing channels

There are many other digital marketing channels and platforms that are profound and worth mentioning, such as:

Mobile marketing, which has become essential due to the growing use of smartphones. It encompasses strategies and tactics aimed at reaching and engaging users on their mobile devices, offering opportunities for real-time engagement and personalization.

2.3.2.1 Mobile applications

Mobile applications offer an immersive, personalized user experience, enabling companies to offer unique features such as loyalty programs, games, augmented reality tools, and push notifications. Mobile applications can be used to boost brand awareness, stimulate engagement and generate sales. They also collect valuable data on user behavior, which can be used to further personalize the experience and improve future marketing campaigns.

2.3.2.2 Mobile-optimized websites

With the majority of web traffic now coming from mobile devices, it's crucial that websites are optimized for smaller screens and slower connections. Mobile-friendly websites offer a seamless user experience, with fast loading times, easy navigation and content tailored to mobile devices. This improves user engagement, reduces bounce rates and increases the chances of conversion.

2.3.2.3 SMS marketing

SMS marketing enables companies to send promotional text messages directly to their customers' cell phones. This method can be very effective for urgent offers, event reminders and exclusive promotions. SMS messages have a high open rate and enable direct, instant communication with customers. However, it's important to use SMS marketing sparingly and in a targeted way to avoid spamming customers.

2.3.2.4 Mobile advertising

Mobile ads can appear in applications, games, websites and search results on mobile devices. They can be targeted according to users' location, demographics, interests and behaviors. Common mobile ad formats include banners, interstitials (full-screen ads that appear between application screens), videos and native ads. Mobile ads can be highly effective in reaching users when they're on the move and more likely to be engaged with their phone.

2.3.3 Digital marketing tools[17]

Digital marketing tools are essential for planning, executing and analyzing marketing campaigns. They enable companies to increase efficiency, reach a wider audience and optimize ROI. Here's a detailed description of some of the most commonly used tools:

2.3.3.1 Data analysis and social media management tools

Data analysis tools are the cornerstone of any successful digital marketing strategy. They enable marketers to collect, measure and interpret data from a variety of sources, such as websites, social media, e-mail campaigns and advertising platforms. These tools provide valuable insights into user behavior, campaign performance, conversion rates and much more. By understanding this data, marketers can make informed decisions, optimize their campaigns and improve their ROI.

2.3.3.1.1 Google Analytics

It's one of the most popular and comprehensive website analytics tools, offering a wealth of reports and features for tracking traffic, engagement and conversions. It enables marketers to understand where their traffic is coming from, how users are navigating their site, which pages are the most popular, and what actions users are taking on the site. Google Analytics also offers advanced features such as conversion funnel analysis, A/B testing and real-time user behavior analysis.

2.3.3.1.2 Adobe Analytics

This enterprise-grade analytics platform offers advanced capabilities for tracking and analyzing data across all digital channels, including websites, mobile apps, social media and email campaigns. Adobe Analytics enables companies to create customized reports, segment their audiences, and gain in-depth insights into the customer journey.

[17] [17] Ryan D.,Russ H. (July 31, 2023), "Digital Marketing For Dummies", 2nd edition, page 321.

2.3.3.1.3 Social media analysis tools

Each social media platform offers its own integrated analytics tools, such as Facebook Insights, Instagram Insights, Twitter Analytics and LinkedIn Analytics. These tools provide data on post performance, user engagement, post reach, and audience demographics. There are also third-party tools, such as Hootsuite Insights, Sprout Social and Buffer Analyze, which consolidate data from multiple social media platforms and provide an overview of social network performance.

2.3.3.1.4 Marketing analysis platforms

These platforms, such as HubSpot, Marketo and Pardot, offer comprehensive marketing analytics capabilities, from lead and campaign tracking to attribution analysis and ROI measurement. They enable marketers to integrate data from different sources, create customized dashboards and generate detailed reports on the performance of their marketing campaigns.

Social media management platforms (SMMPs) are essential tools for companies looking to effectively manage their social media presence. These platforms centralize the management of multiple social media accounts, enabling marketers to schedule posts, monitor brand mentions, interact with subscribers, and analyze the performance of their campaigns.

2.3.3.1.5 Hootsuite

This popular platform offers a user-friendly interface for managing multiple social media accounts, scheduling posts, tracking conversations, and analyzing results. It also offers collaborative features for marketing teams, enabling them to delegate tasks, track approvals and work together on campaigns.

2.3.3.1.6 Buffer

Buffer is another well-known social media management platform, offering similar functionality to Hootsuite. What sets it apart is its focus on planning and optimizing posts to maximize engagement. Buffer offers tools for finding the best time to post, suggesting relevant content, and analyzing post performance.

2.3.3.1.7 Sprout Social

Sprout Social is a more comprehensive platform offering advanced social listening, customer relationship management (CRM) and reporting functionalities. It enables companies to monitor conversations on social networks, respond to comments and messages, and manage customer interactions. Sprout Social also offers tools for analyzing sentiment, identifying influencers and measuring the impact of social network campaigns.

2.3.3.1.8 Later

Later is a platform specialized in planning and scheduling visual content on Instagram, Pinterest and other visual platforms. It offers drag-and-drop functionality to create content calendars, preview posts, and optimize hashtags. Later is a valuable tool for brands that rely on visual marketing to reach their target audience.

2.3.3.2 Email marketing tools

Email marketing remains one of the most effective and profitable digital marketing channels. It enables companies to communicate directly with their subscribers, sending them personalized offers, product updates and relevant content. Well-executed email marketing campaigns can generate leads, boost sales and foster customer loyalty.

2.3.3.2.1 Mailchimp

This popular platform offers an intuitive interface for creating and sending e-mail campaigns, segmenting mailing lists, personalizing messages and automating workflows. Mailchimp also offers professional e-mail templates, A/B testing tools and detailed reporting on campaign performance.

2.3.3.2.2 Constant Contact

Constant Contact is another user-friendly e-mail marketing platform offering similar functionality to Mailchimp. It stands out for its drag-and-drop e-mail creation tools, integrations with social media platforms and event marketing options.

2.3.3.2.3 ActiveCampaign

ActiveCampaign is a more advanced platform offering sophisticated marketing automation features, such as personalized workflows, behavior-based triggers and lead scoring. It's ideal for companies looking to implement complex, personalized e-mail marketing campaigns.

2.3.3.2.4 ConvertKit

ConvertKit is an e-mail marketing platform designed specifically for content creators, bloggers and online entrepreneurs. It offers features to create landing pages, sign-up forms, and automated email sequences to nurture prospects and convert them into customers.

2.3.3.3 Content creation tools

Content is king in the world of digital marketing, and content creation tools are essential for producing high-quality content that attracts and engages the target audience. These tools can include graphic design software, video editors, blogging platforms and SEO tools. By using these tools, marketers can create content that is visually appealing, informative and search engine optimized, improving their brand's visibility and driving more traffic to their website.

2.3.3.3.1 Canva

Canva is an easy-to-use online graphic design tool that enables marketers to create eye-catching visuals for social media, blogs, ads and other marketing materials. It offers an extensive library of templates, images, icons and fonts, as well as simple editing tools for customizing designs.

2.3.3.3.2 Adobe Creative Cloud

This suite of professional creative applications includes Photoshop for image editing, Illustrator for vector graphics, Premiere Pro for video editing, and many more. Adobe Creative Cloud is the benchmark for creative professionals, offering advanced features for producing high-quality content.

2.3.3.3.3 WordPress

is the world's most popular blog and website platform. It offers an intuitive interface for creating and managing content, as well as a vast library of themes and plugins for customizing the look and functionality of a website. WordPress is a powerful tool for businesses wishing to create a professional blog or a complete website.

2.3.3.3.4 SEMrush

SEMrush is an all-in-one SEO tool offering a full range of features for keyword analysis, competitor research, ranking tracking, website auditing and link building. It helps marketers optimize their content for search engines and improve their online visibility.

2.4 Conclusion

In conclusion, this chapter has provided a comprehensive overview of the fundamental concepts, strategies and tools of digital marketing, laying the essential foundations for understanding this constantly evolving field.

We began by exploring the definition and history of digital marketing, tracing its evolution from the early days of database marketing to the current era of sophisticated digital platforms. This historical perspective gave us a better understanding of the foundations on which modern digital marketing is based.

Next, we took an in-depth look at the different types of digital marketing, focusing on both inbound and outbound approaches. This analysis highlighted the diversity of strategies available to marketers, each with its own specific strengths and applications.

Finally, our exploration of digital marketing tools, platforms and channels highlighted the crucial importance of technology in this field. From data analysis tools to social media management platforms, email marketing and content creation solutions, we saw how these resources enable marketers to effectively measure, optimize and execute their strategies.

Ultimately, this chapter has highlighted the multifaceted and dynamic nature of digital marketing. It has underlined the importance for marketing professionals to master not only the fundamental concepts, but also the ever-evolving tools and technologies that shape this field. By embracing this knowledge and staying at the forefront of innovation, companies can truly harness the power of digital marketing to reach and engage their target audiences more effectively than ever before.

MACHINE LEARNING

AND ITS APPLICATION TO DIGITAL MARKETING

CHAPTER III :

► MACHINE LEARNING AND ITS APPLICATION TO DIGITAL MARKETING

3.1 Introduction

Machine learning is at the heart of a veritable revolution in the digital marketing landscape. Once confined to the academic and futuristic spheres, this algorithmic domain powered by massive amounts of data is now profoundly reconfiguring the way brands interact with consumers, optimize their campaigns and drive growth. The text we are about to examine offers a comprehensive analysis of the transformative impact of ML on two fundamental aspects of marketing: customer engagement and marketing performance optimization.

In the first section, the text explores how ML enables unprecedented hyper-personalization of marketing interactions. Thanks to techniques such as granular consumer segmentation, dynamic content adaptation, sophisticated recommendation engines and predictive behavior analysis, brands can now offer tailor-made experiences that respond with surgical precision to individual preferences. ML is also revolutionizing customer engagement via chatbots powered by artificial intelligence and real-time sentiment analysis.

The second section looks at the role of ML in optimizing marketing performance through various applications. These include advanced customer segmentation, multi-channel campaign optimization using multivariate testing and attribution modeling, and ultra-personalized ad targeting made possible by programmatic advertising and real-time bidding.

However, despite these exciting promises, the text warns of the potential harmful effects of indiscriminate ML deployment. A third section analyzes in detail two major pitfalls: the echo chamber effect that could limit new product discovery, and the worrying theory of a "dead Internet" where AI-generated content would render online interactions artificial and undermine consumer trust.

This rich and nuanced analysis of both the exciting and worrying implications of integrating ML into marketing strategies is essential to understanding the real issues at stake in this ongoing technological revolution. By exploring both the promising benefits and the potential risks, this text lays the foundations for much-needed reflection on how to wisely harness the power of ML while preserving consumer authenticity and engagement.

3.2 Machine learning and its application to digital marketing

3.2.1 Machine learning to improve customer engagement

3.2.1.1 Personalizing engagement

Machine learning (ML), once considered a notion confined to academic circles and science fiction, is now a central component of the most advanced digital marketing strategies. This algorithmic field, based on complex mathematical models capable of learning from data, is fueled by vast amounts of information from diverse sources such as user interactions, purchase histories, and online behaviors. Guided by the human ingenuity of data scientists and marketing experts, ML is fundamentally reconfiguring the way brands interact with consumers, optimize campaigns across multiple channels, and drive business growth in an ever-changing digital landscape. This section offers a comprehensive exploration of the various methods by which ML enhances customer engagement, examining in detail the advanced techniques of personalization, predictive analytics, and real-time optimization that are revolutionizing marketing performance optimization in the digital world Hyperpersonalization: constitutes a revolutionary paradigm in digital marketing where interactions with customers are meticulously tailored to their individual preferences and behaviors, going far beyond simple demographic segmentation. This advanced level of personalization, which takes into account a multitude of factors such as purchase history, browsing habits, interests expressed on social networks, and even the user's situational context, is made possible by ML's sophisticated algorithms. These algorithms are able to perform extremely precise granular segmentation and dynamically adapt content in real time, creating unique experiences for each consumer. This tailored approach aims to create more relevant, engaging and memorable interactions at every touchpoint between brand and customer.

3.2.1.1.1 Granular segmentation

ML's algorithms have significantly improved traditional segmentation methods by enabling a fine breakdown of customer databases into micro-segments. This ultra-precise segmentation goes far beyond broad categories based on age, gender or geographical location. It is based on a multitude of complex, interconnected variables, including detailed purchase history (not only what was bought, but also when, where and how), meticulously analyzed browsing behavior (time spent on each page, browsing paths, shopping cart abandonments), social network interactions (likes, shares, comments), in-depth demographic data, elaborate psychographic profiles (attitudes, values, lifestyles) and real-time contextual clues such as precise location, local weather, or even mood inferred from recent interactions. This granular segmentation, made possible by ML's ability to process and analyze massive volumes of heterogeneous data, enables extremely targeted and relevant communication for each individual, increasing the effectiveness of marketing messages by tailoring them to the finest nuances of each consumer's preferences and behaviors.

3.2.1.1.2 Dynamic content adaptation

Thanks to ML, digital platforms such as websites, e-mails and application interfaces can adapt their content, layout and calls to action in real time to the specific data of each user. This dynamic adaptation goes far beyond a simple change of text or image. It involves a complete reconfiguration of the user experience, taking into account not only the user's explicit preferences, but also their implicit behaviors, their history of interactions with the brand, and even contextual factors such as the time of day or the device being used. For example, a travel site can offer different destinations to an experienced traveler than to a novice, by adjusting not only destination recommendations, but also the type of information presented (focus on adventurous activities for the former, on amenities and safety for the latter), the visual style (dynamic images of extreme activities vs. peaceful landscapes), and even the site's navigation structure. This real-time adaptation enhances the relevance and appeal of the content presented, significantly increasing the chances of engagement and conversion.

3.2.1.1.3 Product recommendation engines

Using sophisticated techniques such as collaborative filtering, content-based filtering and hybrid approaches combining several methods, ML-driven recommendation engines generate highly personalized product suggestions. These systems don't just recommend products that are similar to those already purchased or consulted. They deeply analyze user behavior patterns, compare them with those of similar users, and take into account contextual factors such as seasonality, market trends, and even real-time inventory. These engines continually learn from user interactions, refining their recommendations to better match individual preferences, boosting sales and improving the shopping experience. For example, a recommendation engine for a music streaming platform won't just suggest artists from the same genre, but can recommend playlists tailored to the user's inferred mood, activity (work, sport, relaxation), or even local weather.

3.2.1.1.4 Personalized email marketing

ML-powered email marketing platforms enable advanced email personalization, going far beyond simply inserting the recipient's name. These systems are capable of triggering messages based on specific customer behaviors, such as abandoning a shopping cart, repeatedly viewing a product, or reaching a loyalty milestone. They segment mailing lists according to engagement levels, purchase history, and even inferred reading preferences (for example, the propensity to open emails at certain times or on certain days). Personalization extends to subject lines, tailored to maximize open rates according to individual preferences (humorous tone, direct approach, or more formal style), and to the content itself, with images, offers, and even message structures tailored to each recipient. This advanced personalization significantly boosts open and click-through rates, improving the overall effectiveness of email campaigns and strengthening customer relationships over the long term.

3.2.1.2 Predictive customer analysis

Made possible by ML, predictive analysis enables marketers to transform reactive strategies into proactive ones, anticipating consumer needs and behaviors to optimize marketing interventions. This approach goes far beyond the simple analysis of past trends. It uses complex algorithms to identify subtle patterns in the data, take into account a multitude of variables, and generate accurate predictions of future customer behavior. This enables companies to make informed decisions, allocate resources efficiently, and create personalized customer experiences even before the customer expresses a need.

3.2.1.2.1 Churn's prediction

Churn prediction, also known as customer attrition prediction, is a sophisticated process that uses varied data and complex analyses to identify customers likely to stop using a service or product. This approach goes far beyond simply observing declines in usage. It integrates a multitude of factors such as customer service interaction patterns, fluctuations in purchasing habits, changes in engagement on social networks, and even external factors such as market conditions or competing offers. This is a crucial concern for companies, as the cost of acquiring new customers often far exceeds the cost of retaining existing ones. Churn prediction typically involves ML models that analyze customer behavior and engagement data over long periods. These models look for subtle patterns that might indicate that a customer is becoming less satisfied or engaged, long before obvious signs appear. For example, a sudden drop in usage, a change in purchasing behavior or negative feedback could all be indicators of potential churn. By identifying these early signals, companies can implement targeted retention strategies, such as personalized offers, proactive customer support, or tailored loyalty programs, to prevent customer churn.

3.2.1.2.2 Purchase prediction

By analyzing past purchase patterns and browsing behavior, ML models can predict consumers' future purchase decisions with remarkable accuracy. This analysis goes far beyond the simple extrapolation of previous purchases. It incorporates a multitude of factors such as seasonal variations, market trends, inferred life events (such as a move or change of professional situation), and even the influence of social networks on purchasing preferences. This anticipation enables marketers to send highly relevant and timely product recommendations, create cross-selling or up-selling opportunities finely tuned to the customer's anticipated needs, and generate anticipation in customers by presenting products at the most propitious moment in their buying journey. For example, an algorithm could predict that a customer who has recently purchased a tent and consulted hiking guides will be interested in hiking boots in the next few weeks, enabling the brand to present targeted offers before the customer has even begun their search. This proactive approach significantly increases conversion rates by perfectly aligning the offer with the moment when the customer is most likely to make a purchase.

3.2.1.2.3 Modeling the next best action

These sophisticated models, operating in real time, go far beyond simple predefined response scripts. They guide customer service representatives and chatbots by dynamically suggesting the most appropriate answers, solutions or offers to meet customer requests and needs. These models take into account not only the complete history of the customer's interactions with the company, but also contextual factors such as the emotional tone of the current conversation, the customer's communication preferences, and even external events that could influence customer satisfaction. For example, during a call to customer service, the model could suggest that the agent offer specific compensation based on the customer's loyalty history, the nature of their current problem, and previous offers that have been effective for similar customers in comparable situations. This approach not only enhances the customer experience by providing more relevant and personalized solutions, but also improves operational efficiency by enabling agents to make informed decisions more quickly.

3.2.1.2.4 Lead scoring

ML's algorithms analyze a multitude of lead data to assign scores that reflect the likelihood of conversion. This analysis goes far beyond simple demographic data or interaction history. It incorporates subtle behavioral signals such as time spent on certain website pages, frequency and nature of interactions with company content on social networks, responsiveness to previous email campaigns, and even external data such as industry trends or the financial health of the lead's company (for B2B sales). This prioritization enables sales teams to focus their efforts on the most promising leads, adapting their approach according to each lead's score and specific characteristics. For example, a high-scoring lead might be immediately directed to a senior sales representative for personalized follow-up, while a medium-scoring lead might receive a series of automated educational emails before direct contact. This data-driven approach thus improves conversion rates by enabling a more efficient allocation of sales resources, and ensuring that each lead receives the attention and type of interaction most appropriate to their stage in the buying journey.

Chatbots and virtual assistants: thanks to ML, have revolutionized conversational marketing by offering immediate, personalized interactions that improve customer satisfaction and optimize support processes. These tools go far beyond simple automatic response systems based on keywords. They use deep learning algorithms to understand the context, intent and even emotional nuances of customer queries, enabling more natural and productive conversations.

3.2.1.2.5 Natural language understanding

Advanced Natural Language Understanding (NLU) capabilities enable chatbots to understand the subtleties of human language, including slang, idioms and context. This understanding goes beyond simple keyword recognition. It involves deep semantic analysis that captures the real intent behind user queries, even when they are expressed indirectly or ambiguously. For example, a chatbot equipped with advanced NLU can understand that a question like "I can't connect" is not just a statement, but an implicit request for help in solving a connection problem. This ability to interpret natural language in all its complexity promotes more natural and engaging conversations with customers, making interactions more efficient and enjoyable. What's more, by understanding context and linguistic nuances, these chatbots can adapt their tone and communication style to better match that of the user, creating a more personalized and satisfying experience.

3.2.1.2.6 Sentiment analysis in conversations

Chatbots equipped with sentiment analysis can assess customer emotions in real time, going far beyond the simple detection of positive or negative words. These advanced systems analyze a multitude of linguistic and contextual indicators to deduce the customer's emotional state, including word choice, sentence structure, punctuation, and even the pace of the conversation. This ability enables them to adjust their responses appropriately, modulating the tone, style and content of their messages to better respond to the customer's emotional state. For example, faced with a frustrated customer, the chatbot might adopt a more empathetic tone, offer a sincere apology, and propose a quick resolution to the problem. On the other hand, with an enthusiastic customer, it might adopt a more playful tone and seize the opportunity to suggest complementary products or services. What's more, these systems are able to detect early signs of dissatisfaction or confusion, enabling problems to be escalated to human agents if necessary, before the situation deteriorates. This ability to react empathetically and contextually to customer emotions helps deliver a more human, personalized and satisfying customer experience, strengthening the relationship between brand and consumer.

3.2.1.2.7 Omnichannel integration

Modern chatbots are integrated across a variety of platforms, including messaging apps, social networks and voice assistants, delivering a consistent, seamless customer support experience, whatever channel the customer chooses. This integration goes far beyond a simple presence on multiple platforms. It involves real-time synchronization of data and interactions across all channels, enabling seamless continuity of the customer experience. For example, a customer could start a conversation on the company's website, continue it via the mobile app while on the move, and end it with a phone call, without having to repeat their information or query history. Omnichannel chatbots can access the customer's complete interaction history, regardless of the channel previously used, and adapt their approach accordingly. This omnichannel integration not only ensures consistency in customer support, but also improves efficiency by enabling faster problem resolution and delivering a smoother, more personalized customer experience.

3.2.1.2.8 Proactive engagement

Chatbots can proactively initiate conversations based on customer behavior on websites or applications, going beyond simply responding to explicit requests. These advanced systems analyze in real time a multitude of behavioral signals, such as time spent on certain pages, mouse movements, products consulted, or even hesitations in the purchasing process. Based on these analyses, chatbots can intervene in a timely and contextual manner. For example, if a user spends an unusual amount of time on a page, the chatbot could offer personalized assistance. Or, if a customer adds several items to their basket but is hesitant to finalize the purchase, the chatbot could intervene to offer additional product information, reviews from other customers, or even special offers to encourage conversion. This proactive approach increases engagement, offers personalized recommendations, and improves conversion rates by providing relevant, timely information exactly when the customer needs it most. What's more, by anticipating customer needs, this approach can significantly improve customer satisfaction and reinforce the perception of the brand as attentive and responsive.

Sentiment analysis: via ML, is a crucial tool enabling brands to understand and respond to customer emotions, feedback and trends in real time. This technology goes far beyond simply categorizing comments as positive or negative. It provides a nuanced and contextual understanding of the feelings expressed by consumers across various channels.

3.2.1.2.9 Large-scale social listening

ML-powered social listening tools can monitor vast quantities of social network posts, reviews and online discussions, processing millions of mentions in real time. These systems don't just count positive or negative mentions. They use sophisticated algorithms to analyze context, detect sarcasm, understand linguistic and cultural nuances, and even interpret emojis and memes. By analyzing this data, brands can assess overall sentiment with unprecedented accuracy, track competitor mentions for detailed comparative analysis, and identify emerging trends before they even become mainstream. For example, a social listening tool could detect growing dissatisfaction with a specific aspect of a product, enabling the brand to react quickly before the problem escalates. Or it could identify an unexpected new use for a product among a segment of consumers, opening up new marketing opportunities. This large-scale, real-time analysis capability enables brands to stay ahead of market trends, anticipate consumer needs, and rapidly adapt their marketing and product development strategies.

3.2.2 Machine learning for optimized marketing performance[18]

3.2.2.1 Customer segmentation

While Recency, Frequency and Monetary Value analysis remains a valuable tool for segmenting customers, it has certain limitations in terms of depth of analysis. Machine learning (ML) algorithms make it possible to go far beyond these traditional parameters by integrating a much wider range of variables. These variables include psychographic data, which captures consumer attitudes, values, and interests, detailed online behavior, social networking activities, and even data from external sources such as credit bureaus and third-party data providers. This integration enables the creation of hyper-targeted segments that reflect not only customers' transactional behaviors, but also their deeper, contextual

[18] [19] Andrea De M., Andrea S., Andrea Ba. (June 24, 2022), "Machine learning and artificial intelligence use in marketing: a general taxonomy". https://link.springer.com/article/10.1007/s43039-022-00057-w

motivations. As a result, marketing campaigns can be designed more strategically and precisely, improving the relevance of messages and the effectiveness of interventions.

3.2.2.1.1 Look-alike modeling

Lookalike modeling exploits the advanced capabilities of ML to identify new prospects with similar characteristics to your most valuable customers. This technique relies on analyzing the demographic, behavioral and psychographic data of your existing customer base to find "lookalikes" among larger databases of potential prospects. By targeting these lookalikes, marketers can effectively extend their reach by focusing on audiences with a high probability of conversion, optimizing marketing resources and increasing the ROI of advertising campaigns.

3.2.2.1.2 Predicting customer value

Customer Lifetime Value prediction (CLTV) is another crucial application of ML in marketing. ML models can analyze tons of historical and behavioral data to estimate the future value of each customer over their entire lifecycle. This enables marketers to segment customers according to their predictive value and allocate resources more strategically. Customers with a high CLTV can benefit from personalized treatments, exclusive loyalty programs and special offers, while customers with a lower CLTV can be targeted by less expensive but equally effective campaigns. This approach not only maximizes the profitability of marketing investments, but also improves customer satisfaction and loyalty.

3.2.2.1.3 Dynamic segmentation

Consumer behavior is constantly evolving in response to a multitude of internal and external factors. ML's algorithms enable dynamic, real-time segmentation, where customer segments are continually updated according to new behavioral and transactional data. This ability to adapt quickly to changes in customer preferences and behaviors ensures that marketing strategies remain relevant and effective. For example, a promotional campaign can be adjusted instantly to target customers who show a sudden interest in a specific product, thus increasing the chances of conversion.

3.2.2.2 Campaign optimization

Traditional A/B testing, while useful, is limited because it can only compare two versions of an element at a time. In contrast, ML-driven multivariate testing enables the simultaneous testing of multiple variations of ads, emails, landing pages, or even entire campaigns. This approach speeds up the optimization process by revealing complex interactions between different campaign elements. For example, a multivariate test could analyze the performance of various combinations of headlines, images and calls-to-action, identifying the most effective combination for each customer segment.

3.2.2.2.1 Dynamic creative optimization

Dynamic creative optimization uses ML algorithms to customize creative elements of ads in real time. This means that components such as headlines, images and calls-to-action can be dynamically adjusted according to each user's specific data. For example, a user browsing a travel site might see ads for tropical destinations if detected as having an interest in beach vacations, while another user might see offers for mountain vacations. This real-time personalization increases relevance and engagement, improving the performance of advertising campaigns.

3.2.2.2.2 Attribution modeling

ML-based attribution modeling goes beyond the last-click attribution model to provide a more comprehensive view of the impact of each touchpoint on the customer journey. By analyzing the multiple and complex interactions between different stages of the buying journey, ML-based attribution models can more accurately attribute credit to different marketing channels. This enables marketers to understand the relative effectiveness of each channel and reallocate budgets more strategically to maximize the overall impact of marketing campaigns.

3.2.2.2.3 Predictive bid optimization

In the field of paid advertising, predictive bid optimization is a key application of ML. Algorithms can analyze user data in real time to predict the conversion probability of each ad impression. Based on these predictions, bidding strategies can be automatically adjusted to maximize the return on advertising investment. For example, an ad campaign can adjust its bids for impressions with a higher probability of conversion, thus reducing unnecessary ad spend and increasing overall campaign effectiveness.

3.2.2.3 Targeting and bidding

3.2.2.3.1 Programmatic advertising

Programmatic advertising is an automated ad buying process that uses ML algorithms to target specific audiences based on a wide range of criteria, such as demographics, interests, online behavior, and real-time contextual data. This automation makes it possible to deliver more relevant ads and improve the effectiveness of advertising campaigns in real time. For example, an advertising campaign for a new car can specifically target users who have recently consulted car comparison websites, or who have shown an interest in similar models on social networks.

3.2.2.3.2 Real-time auctions

Real-time bidding (RTB) platforms use ML to analyze huge amounts of data in milliseconds, enabling advertisers to bid on ad impressions in real time. This ability to make bidding decisions instantly ensures that ads are delivered to the most relevant audiences at the most opportune time, maximizing the effectiveness of ad spend. For example, an RTB campaign can adjust its bids in real time according to the probability of conversion, thus optimizing advertising budgets and improving ROI.

3.2.2.3.3 Fraud detection s

Ad fraud detection is an essential application of ML, helping to protect advertising budgets against fraudulent clicks and impressions. ML algorithms can identify suspicious behavior patterns and prevent fraud in real time, ensuring that advertising resources are used efficiently and campaigns reach their true target audience. This fraud protection is crucial to maintaining the integrity and effectiveness of advertising campaigns.

3.2.2.3.4 Brand safety

Brand safety is another area where ML plays a key role. ML algorithms can analyze the content and context of websites and applications to ensure that ads are not served alongside inappropriate or harmful content. This ensures that ads are delivered in safe environments, protecting brand reputation and avoiding unwanted associations that could damage corporate image.

3.3 Machine learning and digital marketing: the outlook

3.3.1 The potential positive horizon of digital marketing

As machine learning continues to evolve rapidly, its potential to transform the digital marketing landscape is both exhilarating and daunting. This section explores the positive outcomes that ML could bring, promising a future where marketing will be more personalized, efficient and impactful than ever before.

3.3.1.1 The age of hyper-individuation

3.3.1.1.1 A deep understanding of individual consumers

ML's algorithms will become capable of understanding individual consumers at an unprecedented level, exploring their values, emotions and aspirations. This detailed understanding will enable the creation of hyper-personalized experiences, going far beyond simple product recommendations. For example, a user with a passion for adventure travel could receive personalized advice on equipment, itineraries and local guides, enriching every interaction. This capacity for individuation will enable every touchpoint in the customer journey to be transformed so that it responds specifically to the needs and preferences of each consumer, thus improving customer satisfaction and loyalty.

3.3.1.1.2 Dynamic and narrative campaigns

Marketing campaigns will become dynamic narratives, adapting in real time to user interactions and feedback. This narrative approach enables deeper engagement and stronger emotional connections between brands and consumers. For example, a product launch campaign could evolve according to consumer reactions on social networks, continually adjusting content and messages to better resonate with the target audience. This adaptability will not only improve campaign effectiveness, but also create memorable and engaging brand experiences.

3.3.1.1.3 AI-driven virtual influencers and brand ambassadors

AI-driven virtual influencers and brand ambassadors will become commonplace, offering personalized recommendations and interactions that blur the boundaries between human and machine interaction. These virtual entities, endowed with unique personalities and voices, will be able to engage consumers authentically and continuously, strengthening customer loyalty and satisfaction. For example, a virtual influencer could interact with users on social networks, offering personalized advice and product recommendations based on users' individual preferences and past behavior.

3.3.1.2 Marketing automation amplified

ML will automate increasingly complex marketing tasks, freeing up human marketers to focus on strategy and creativity. For example, email marketing campaigns could be fully automated, from segmentation to message personalization to optimal timing of sends. This advanced automation will enable more complex campaigns to be managed with greater precision and efficiency, optimizing marketing resources.

3.3.1.2.1 AI-driven content generation tools

AI-driven content generation tools will produce high-quality blog posts, social network updates and even video scripts, all tailored to specific audiences and precise objectives. These tools will enable marketers to maintain a constant flow of engaging content without overloading human resources. For example, a content generation tool could create SEO-optimized blog posts based on the topics most relevant and sought-after by the target audience.

3.3.1.2.2 Sophisticated predictive analysis

Predictive analytics will become even more sophisticated, enabling marketers to anticipate customer needs and proactively address them with personalized offers and solutions. For example, an online retailer could predict which products a customer is likely to buy next, and offer recommendations before they even start looking. This ability to anticipate customer needs will create smoother, more satisfying customer experiences, boosting conversion rates and customer loyalty.

3.3.1.3 Enhanced data confidentiality and security

Advances in ML will lead to more robust data privacy and security measures, ensuring that consumer data is handled responsibly and ethically. For example, differential privacy techniques will enable marketers to gain valuable insights without compromising individual privacy. These techniques will add statistical noise to the data, making individual information undetectable while preserving the overall analytical value.

3.3.1.3.1 Differential confidentiality techniques

Differential privacy techniques will enable marketers to extract valuable insights from data without compromising individual confidentiality. For example, a company could analyze global purchasing trends without accessing each customer's specific data, thus guaranteeing the confidentiality of personal data while gaining useful insights for marketing strategy.

3.3.1.3.2 Fraud detection and prevention

ML algorithms will be deployed to detect and prevent fraud, protecting both consumers and businesses. For example, real-time monitoring systems will be able to identify suspicious transactions and take immediate action to avoid financial loss. This ability to prevent fraud in real time is crucial to maintaining consumer confidence and protecting corporate resources.

3.3.2 The potential pitfalls of machine learning in digital marketing

While the future of machine learning (ML) in digital marketing holds immense promise, it's crucial to recognize the potential negative outcomes that could arise if it's not carefully managed. This section explores in detail the challenges and potential pitfalls associated with integrating ML into digital marketing strategies.

3.3.2.1 The echo chamber effect[19]

As machine learning algorithms become more adept at personalization, they risk creating environments where consumers are primarily exposed to content that reinforces their existing preferences and behaviors. This increased personalization may seem beneficial in the short term, but it carries significant risks for marketing in the long term.

When people are continually exposed to information and products that confirm their preferences, they can become less receptive to new ideas and products. This phenomenon, often referred to as the "echo chamber effect", limits consumers' ability to discover new brands, products or services. In marketing, this can lead to market saturation, where consumers see only the same types of products and messages, reducing their propensity to explore and try new offerings.

3.3.2.1.1 Reducing the diversity of products and services

Echo chambers can also reduce the diversity of products and services that consumers consider. Algorithms, based on past preferences, may only suggest products similar to those that consumers have already purchased or viewed. This limits the discovery of innovative or niche products, harming market diversity.

3.3.2.1.2 Stagnation and lack of innovation

For companies, excessive personalization can lead to stagnation. If algorithms continue to push the same types of products to a group of consumers,

[19] [20] Berg A., Provins S., Silberman G., White K., (31 May 2021), "artificial intelligence and echo chambers". https://www.counterterrorismgroup.com/post/artificial-intelligence-and-echo-chambers

opportunities to introduce innovations or differentiated products are reduced. This can make it difficult for companies to launch new products or enter new market segments.

3.3.2.2 The dead internet theory[20]

The Dead Internet theory, a concept that has gained ground in recent years, postulates a frightening hypothesis: a significant proportion of online content is not created by humans, but rather by sophisticated artificial intelligence (AI) algorithms. While this theory often falls into the realms of speculation and conspiracy, it raises profound questions about the authenticity of online interactions and the future of digital marketing.

3.3.2.2.1 The erosion of authenticity in the digital age

At the heart of Dead Internet theory lies a fundamental concern about the erosion of authenticity in the digital realm. As AI-generated content becomes increasingly sophisticated, blurring the boundaries between human and machine-generated expression, the very notion of authenticity is being called into question. This poses a major challenge to digital marketers, who rely on building trust and establishing genuine connections with their audiences.

In a world where AI-generated social media posts, product reviews and even news articles are becoming indistinguishable from human-created content, how can brands differentiate themselves and retain their unique voice?

How can consumers trust the information they encounter online if they can't discern whether it comes from a human or a machine?

3.3.2.2.2 Implications for consumer trust and commitment

Consumer trust is a precious commodity in the digital age. It's the foundation on which successful brands are built. If consumers can't trust the authenticity of

[20] [21] Butler S. (Mar 8, 2024), "What Is the Dead Internet Theory?". https://www.howtogeek.com/what-is-the-dead-internet-theory/

online content, their trust in brands and institutions could erode, leading to lower engagement, lower conversion rates and, ultimately, a loss of brand loyalty.

Dead Internet theory suggests that as AI-generated content proliferates, consumers may become increasingly skeptical of online information. They may question the motivations behind seemingly authentic posts on social networks, doubt the veracity of online reviews and become less receptive to marketing messages that appear to be generated by algorithms rather than humans.

What's more, if consumers perceive that brands are using AI to manipulate or deceive them, this could backfire spectacularly, leading to a backlash against the brand and long-term damage to its reputation.

3.3.2.2.3 The paradox of personalization

Ironically, the rise of AI-generated content is closely linked to the quest for personalization, the cornerstone of modern digital marketing. ML algorithms are used to analyze vast quantities of data in order to tailor content, recommendations and experiences to individual users. However, Dead Internet theory suggests that this personalization could contribute to the problem of inauthenticity.

As algorithms become more adept at mimicking human behavior and preferences, the content they generate may become increasingly indistinguishable from human-created content. This could lead to a paradoxical situation where personalization, intended to enhance the customer experience, inadvertently contributes to the erosion of trust and authenticity.

3.4 Conclusion

Ultimately, the meteoric rise of machine learning in the digital marketing landscape represents both a fascinating opportunity and a daunting challenge. As we've explored, ML has the potential to radically transform the way brands interact with their audiences, ushering in an era of hyper-personalization, deep engagement and unprecedented optimization of marketing campaigns.

However, it would be naïve to blindly embrace this technological revolution without carefully considering its long-term implications. The pitfalls of the echo chamber effect and the "dead Internet" remind us that the quest for relevance and marketing efficiency must not come at the expense of authenticity and trust - fundamental pillars on which lasting relationships between brands and consumers rest.

So, as we enter this new era, it will be up to marketing professionals to strike a delicate balance. They will need to wisely harness the power of ML to deliver truly personalized and engaging experiences, while preserving an authentic connection with their audience. A measured, ethical and responsible approach to integrating ML into marketing strategies will be essential.

Rather than being blinded by the promises of the latest technological innovations, the wisest brand managers will recognize that ML is merely a powerful tool, designed to amplify - not replace - the human expertise, creativity and intelligence that underpin successful marketing. By embracing this nuanced vision, they can truly harness the revolutionary potential of ML while preserving the soul and authenticity of their brands.

MACHINE LEARNING: APPLICATION TO WEB AD CLICK PREDICTION

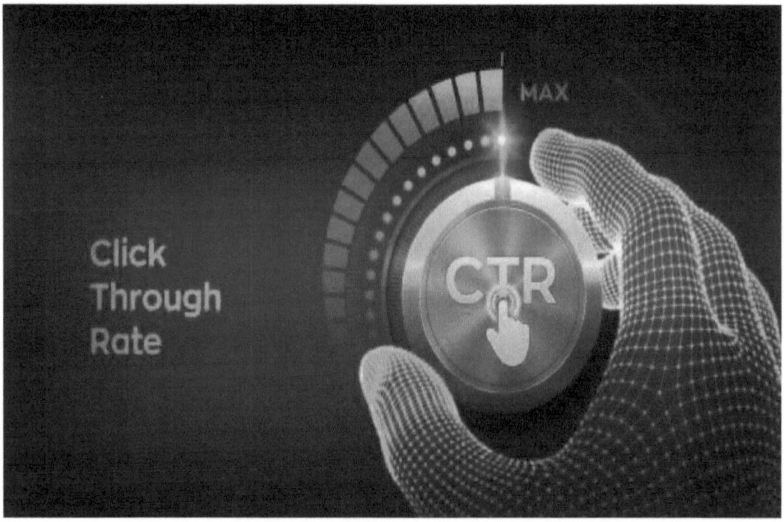

CHAPTER V :

▶MACHINE LEARNING: FOR CLICK PREDICTION ON WEB ADVERTISING

4.1 Introduction

In today's data-driven era, digital marketing has emerged as a strategic force for companies keen to connect with their target audience in a relevant and effective way. However, to take full advantage of this powerful tool, a thorough understanding of consumer behaviors and preferences is essential. This is where machine learning, a revolutionary branch of artificial intelligence, comes in.

This chapter explores the integration of machine learning in digital marketing in depth, focusing on a crucial use case: predicting clicks on online ads. We begin by bringing together the tools and libraries essential for this task, including Python, Pandas, NumPy, Matplotlib and Scikit-learn. These resources form the solid foundation on which we'll build our machine learning model.

Next, we'll dive into data preparation, a crucial step that determines the quality and accuracy of our model. We'll take a detailed look at the AVAZU dataset, a rich source of information on users' interactions with online ads. We will explore data processing techniques, such as cleaning, segmentation and transformation, to ensure that our data is ready for model training.

Once the foundations have been laid, we'll get down to the nitty-gritty of building and training our machine learning model. We'll explore the process of selecting an appropriate algorithm, highlighting the importance of choosing an approach suited to the nature of our data and our specific goal. We will then follow the crucial steps of dividing the data into training and test sets, training the model and evaluating its performance.

Finally, we will analyze the results obtained in depth, highlighting the practical implications and potential benefits of integrating machine learning into digital marketing strategies. We'll explore how insights from our model can be used to optimize advertising campaigns, maximize revenue and improve overall ad performance.

In sum, this chapter offers a holistic perspective on the application of machine learning in digital marketing, focusing on a concrete, practical case study. By combining theoretical concepts with a practical approach, we aim to provide readers with an in-depth understanding of how these two complementary fields can reinforce each other, opening up new avenues to more targeted, effective and profitable marketing strategies.

4.2 Framing the problem

Outbound marketing, while useful for brand awareness, faces challenges such as ad blocking and low engagement.

Traditional outbound marketing strategies, while reaching a wide audience, come up against several obstacles:

4.2.1 Reduced range

Ad-blocking technologies significantly reduce the number of users exposed to ads.

4.2.2 Low commitment

Even when seen, ads often fail to capture users' interest, resulting in low click-through rates (CTR).

4.2.3 Ineffective targeting

Outbound marketing often lacks precise targeting, leading to wasted resources on uninterested audiences.

These limitations hamper the effectiveness of outbound marketing campaigns.

4.3 The proposed solution

This book proposes a solution using a logistic regression model to predict user clicks on ads.

Efficiency poses the implementation of a logistic regression model to improve the effectiveness of outbound marketing. Logistic regression is an ideal statistical method for binary classification tasks. In this case, our objective is to predict whether a user will click (1) or not (0) on an ad.

The model will be trained on historical data containing user characteristics and their corresponding click behavior. These characteristics may include:

✓ Demographic data (age, location, income)

✓ Browsing behavior (previous clicks, website visits)

✓ Online interests (themes, engagement on social networks)

By analyzing these characteristics, the model learns to identify patterns associated with user clicks. It can then predict the likelihood of a new user clicking on a specific ad based on their profile.

4.3.1 The choice of regression

The choice of logistic regression for this book is not insignificant. Several factors justify this selection over other classification models:

4.3.1.1 Binary output

Logistic regression excels in binary classification tasks, where the target variable can take only two values (click = 1 or no click = 0). Our objective is to predict the probability of a click, which perfectly matches the ability of logistic regression to provide output in the form of probabilities between 0 and 1.

4.3.1.2 Interoperability

Logistic regression is appreciated for its relative simplicity and ease of interpretation. The model's coefficients enable us to identify the user characteristics that have the greatest impact on click probability. This understanding of key factors is crucial for optimizing marketing campaigns and targeting the most receptive audiences.

4.3.1.3 Performance

Logistic regression is a robust and efficient algorithm, capable of producing accurate results with reasonably sized data sets. Its relative simplicity makes it less prone to overlearning than more complex models, which is important for guaranteeing the generalizability of predictions to new users.

4.3.1.4 Ethical data collection

Obtaining relevant data to train our logistic regression model raises crucial ethical and legal issues. It is imperative to implement collection methods that respect user privacy and comply with current regulations. Several approaches can be envisaged:

4.3.1.5 Explicit consent

Implementation of an opt-in system where users voluntarily agree to share their data for the purpose of improving advertising targeting. This approach guarantees transparency and respect for user choice.

4.3.1.6 Data anonymization

Use of robust anonymization techniques to remove all personally identifiable information prior to analysis. This method preserves confidentiality while maintaining the statistical value of the data.

4.3.1.7 Data aggregation

Work on aggregate data rather than individual profiles. This approach reduces the risk of re-identification, while enabling the identification of general trends.

4.3.1.8 Ethical partnerships

Collaborate with third-party platforms that already collect user data ethically, ensuring that these partners comply with strict data protection standards.

4.3.1.9 Transparency and control

Provide users with a clear interface enabling them to view the data collected about them, and to modify or delete this information at any time.

These methods, combined with rigorous data governance and regular audits, provide the information needed to drive the model while respecting ethical and legal privacy principles. It is crucial to maintain a balance between the effectiveness of advertising targeting and respect for users' fundamental rights to data confidentiality.

4.4 Tool assembly and data preparation

4.4.1 Assembling the necessary tools[21]

4.4.1.1 Software choices

In this in-depth segment, we take a close look at the crucial steps involved in developing a machine learning model. The function of this model will be to predict the probability of clicks on online advertisements. Building this model requires a thorough understanding of algorithms and their practical application. Python, with its intuitive nature and clear syntax, proves to be the ideal programming language.

The Python ecosystem, enriched by libraries such as scikit-learn, TensorFlow and PyTorch, offers advanced tools for data processing, feature engineering, model selection, hyperparameter optimization and performance evaluation. These libraries are designed to facilitate the task of data scientists, enabling them to model accurate predictions while efficiently managing the large, complex data often associated with advertising campaigns.

[21] [22] Arranz M. I. (Mar 12, 2024), "Data science library hub". https://github.com/imarranz/data-science-library-hub

4.4.1.2 The libraries used

In programming, a library is a collection of pre-written code that programmers can use to optimize certain tasks. These sets of reusable code are often designed to solve common problems, enabling developers to build applications more efficiently and consistently. Libraries are like toolboxes filled with various components that can be integrated into software projects, simplifying the development process and promoting better code management.

For the purposes of our book, we will be using the following libraries:

4.4.1.2.1 Pandas

Pandas is an essential software library for the Python programming language, specially designed to meet the needs of data manipulation and analysis. It provides advanced data structures such as DataFrames and Series, which are powerful tools for managing tabular data and time series. These structures make it easy to perform complex operations on data, such as cleansing, transformation, aggregation and visualization. Pandas is particularly appreciated in the data science community for its ability to work with data from different sources and formats.

4.4.1.2.2 NumPy

NumPy stands for 'Numerical Python'. At the heart of its functionality are multidimensional arrays, meticulously structured collections of data elements. Unlike conventional Python lists, which can accommodate a heterogeneous combination of data types, NumPy arrays impose uniformity, optimizing storage efficiency and facilitating streamlined operations. This library offers a comprehensive suite of tools specifically designed for array manipulation. These include mathematical functions, table formatting techniques and element-by-element operations.

4.4.1.2.3 MatPlotLib

MatPlotLib is specially designed for the creation of a wide range of data visualizations. It enables users to generate a wide variety of plots and graphs, from simple line diagrams to complex interactive displays. Matplotlib has developed into a versatile tool, indispensable for anyone wishing to communicate data through compelling visuals. Its functionality extends beyond simple representation, enabling detailed customization and enhancement of graphical presentations.

4.4.1.2.4 Scikit-learn

Scikit-learn is a machine learning library for Python, renowned for its wide range of algorithms and tools for data mining and data analysis. It is particularly noted for its ease of use and accessibility, making it an ideal choice for both novices and experienced machine learning practitioners. The library includes a wide range of functionalities, from data pre-processing, cross-validation and feature selection to the implementation of various machine learning algorithms such as clustering, classification and regression.

4.4.1.3 Choosing an integrated development environment

An integrated development environment (IDE) is a software application that centralizes the tools essential to software development. An IDE typically combines a source code editor, build automation tools and a debugger in a unified graphical user interface (GUI). This integration facilitates the developer's tasks by providing a unified platform for writing, testing and debugging code. In our case, we'll be using Visual Studio Code (VSCode), a highly extensible and easy-to-use IDE. However, there are other options such as IntelliJ IDEA, Eclipse and NetBeans, each offering unique features and tools tailored to different programming needs and preferences.

4.4.2 Data preparation - AVAZU

4.4.2.1 Data processing

In this part of our chapter, we focus on the crucial choice of a dataset for our machine learning model. Normally, this step requires a painstaking data collection effort to gather the necessary information. However, in our case and to speed up the process, we will base our model on publicly available datasets. This method not only saves time, but also allows us to take advantage of a wealth of pre-processed and structured data, which can considerably improve the robustness and accuracy of our model.

4.4.2.2 The selected data set

The AVAZU dataset, used in a Ka g gle competition[22] , is a rich source for click-through rate (CTR) prediction, comprising 10 days of click-through data, ordered chronologically. It presents a realistic challenge in the field of ad click prediction due to its high volume and the real-world complexity of its features, such as ad content and user interaction details. The choice of AVAZU data for our machine learning model provides a solid foundation for developing sophisticated predictive algorithms. Its comprehensive nature enables us to explore and model the complex patterns that drive user engagement with digital ads.

The AVAZU data set contains the following columns:

- ✓ id: ad identifier
- ✓ click: clicks on the ad with a Boolean value (0/1)
- ✓ hour: format of AA-MM-JJ-HH
- ✓ C1: anonymized categorical variable
- ✓ banner_pos
- ✓ site_id
- ✓ site_domain
- ✓ site_category
- ✓ app_id
- ✓ app_domain
- ✓ app_category

---

[22] [23] Wang S., Cukierski W. (2014). "Click-Through Rate Prediction." https://kaggle.com/competitions/avazu-ctr-prediction

✓ device_id

✓ device_ip

✓ device_model

✓ device_type

✓ device_conn_type

✓ C14-C21: anonymized categorical variables

4.4.2.3 Information processing

We're now embarking on a crucial phase of our book: importing the essential libraries that will serve as the foundation for our data analysis and modeling.

```
import pandas

import numpy

import sklearn

import matplotlib

from matplotlib import pyplot

from sklearn import linear_model
```

After downloading the data set, we notice that it is of considerable size-a staggering 5 gigabytes. This presents a practical challenge in terms of data handling and processing. To remedy this, we'll start our data processing by dividing the data into readable chunks. Leveraging the capabilities of Pandas, we will simplify this process, ensuring that each segment is of sufficient size for efficient analysis without compromising the integrity of our data.

By setting the chunksize parameter to 5 million records, we take a strategic approach to dividing the data set into more manageable chunks, each around 700 megabytes in size.

```
for i,chunk in enumerate(pandas.read_csv('train.csv', chunksize=5000000)):
```

```
chunk.to_csv('chunk{}.csv'.format(i), index=False)
```

Having broken down our data into assimilable segments, we'll now concentrate on importing our CSV file. This will be followed by a painstaking pruning process, where we eliminate all superfluous columns that don't contribute to our analysis. This refinement is crucial, as it simplifies our data, ensuring that only the most relevant information is retained for the development of our machine learning model.

```
data = pandas.read_csv("chunk0.csv",sep=",");

data = data[

["click","C1","hour","banner_pos","device_type","device_conn_type","C14","C15",
"C16","C17","C18","C19","C20","C21"]];
```

After completing the segmentation and cleaning of our data, we successfully loaded and split the data. It is now ready for the training phase. This preparation lays the foundations for the complex task of training the model, paving the way for the development of a predictive algorithm that is both accurate and efficient.

4.5 Building and analyzing the machine learning model

4.5.1 Building the model

4.5.1.1 The algorithmic choice

In the initial phase of our machine learning book, we will identify an optimal algorithm to meet our specific needs. The selection of a suitable algorithm is essential, as it underpins the model's ability to generate accurate predictions. To aid in the model selection process, we will use Matplotlib to construct a scatter plot, which will enable us to critically examine the distribution of the data:

```
pyplot.scatter(data["C14"],data["click"])

pyplot.xlabel = "x"

pyplot.ylabel = "y"
```

pyplot.show()

Executing these commands on a few variables in our data gives the following results:

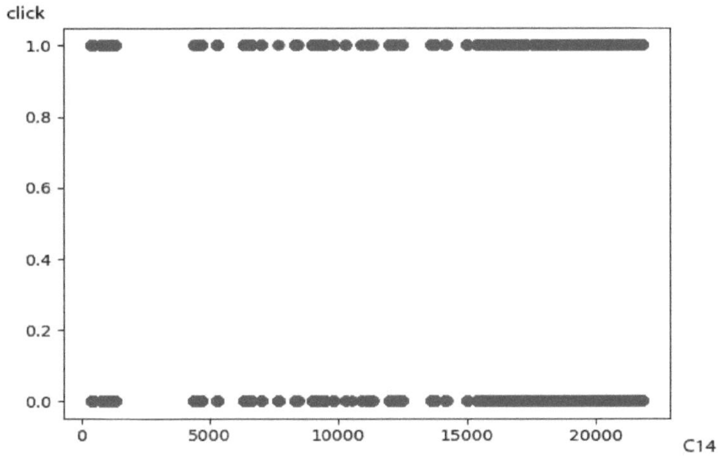

Figure 5Point cloud of clicks on C14

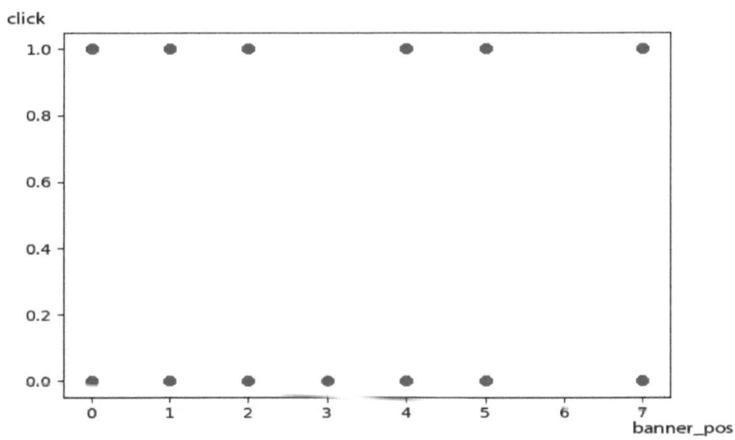

Figure 6Scatterplot of clicks on banner_pos

Looking at the scatterplot, we see that the variable, 'clicks', is binary in nature, taking values of 0 or 1. This dichotomy in the data suggests that logistic regression is the most appropriate method for our predictive model. Logistic regression is competent at handling binary outcomes and can provide probabilities that a given entry point belongs to a certain class, which in this case is the probability that a click is 0 or 1. See the figure below for a demonstration :

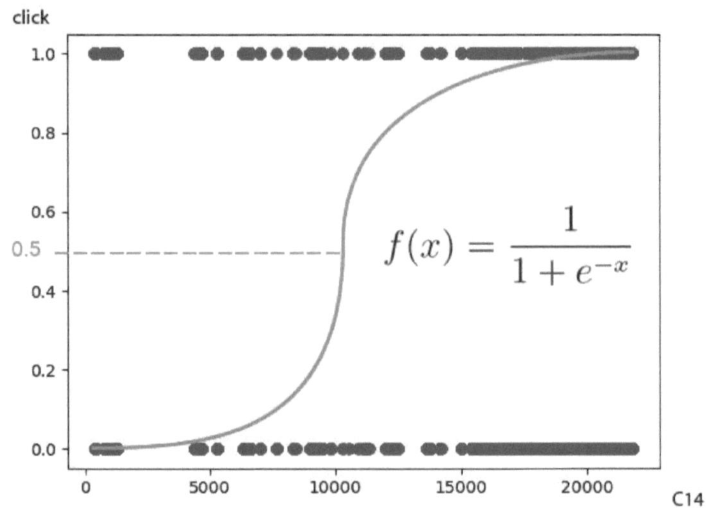

Figure 7Visualization of the logistic regression algorithm on the data

4.5.1.2 Building the model

In the field of machine learning model development, a rigorous and structured approach to data division is paramount. Our data is divided into two subsets: a training subset, which forms the majority, and a validation subset. The training subset is used to train the model, teaching it to make predictions from the input features. The validation subset, containing the binary target variable 'clicks', is hidden from the model during training. This subset is crucial for assessing the model's predictive accuracy on unfamiliar data, thus verifying the model's usefulness in real-life situations. This deliberate partitioning is essential to prevent over-fitting and to confirm the model's predictive reliability.

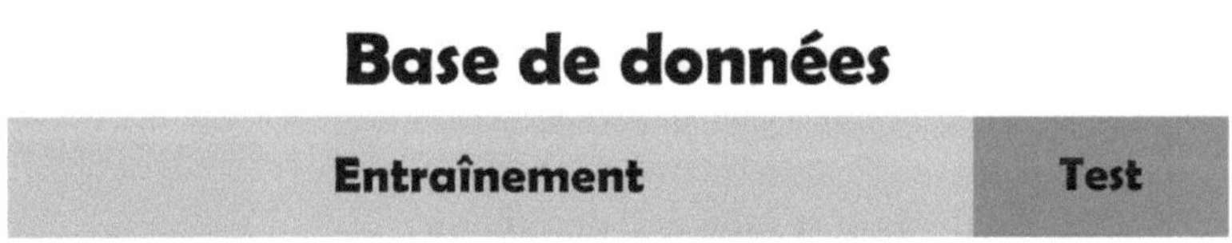

Figure 8Data separation in training and testing

Having established that logistic regression is the appropriate method for our binary classification task, we will now proceed to implement it by coding. The value 0.1 designates the proportion of data, specifically 10%, that we will reserve for testing our model. Also, 'Y' represents the variable 'clicks', which is the outcome we seek to predict. It is the focal point of our logistic regression model. On the other hand, 'X' encompasses all the other data, serving as a set of explanatory variables that will help us understand the factors influencing the occurrence of clicks:

```
predict = "click"

Model = linear_model.LogisticRegression()

X = numpy.array(data.drop([predict],axis=1))

Y = numpy.array(data[predict])

x_train, x_test, y_train, y_test = sklearn.model_selection.train_test_split(X,Y, test_size = 0.1)
```

And to start training our model, we'll run the following command:

```
Model.fit(x_train,y_train)
```

The training phase of our model is likely to be fairly long, particularly in view of the large size of the data. This time is necessary for the model to learn thoroughly. Once training is complete, we can evaluate the model's performance by obtaining its score on the test data using the code provided below:

```
acc = Model.score(x_test, y_test)
```

```
print(acc*100)
```

Our model achieved an accuracy of around 82%. This is a promising result that merits further analysis, which we'll undertake in the next part of our discussion.

4.5.2 Analysis of results and deductions

We have determined that the accuracy of our model is 82%. This level of accuracy indicates that our machine learning model is quite accurate, validating the effort invested in its development. The fact that the model was able to correctly predict 82% of the test data, which was not exposed to it during training, underlines its effectiveness.

In fact, a realization with an accuracy of 82% is clearly superior to a chance level of 50%. This comparison highlights the predictive power of the model and the value it brings compared to a random guess. This model can help us in a number of ways, such as :

4.5.2.1 Optimizing advertising campaigns

- ✓ By leveraging the information in our model, we can fine-tune our advertising campaigns to focus on ads with the highest potential click-through rates.
- ✓ This optimization process involves analyzing patterns and trends that correlate with successful advertising engagement.

4.5.2.2 Maximizing advertising revenues:

- ✓ Strategic placement of high-performance ads in key positions can significantly increase visibility and, consequently, revenues.
- ✓ Understanding user engagement metrics allows us to place ads where they are most likely to be clicked, improving ROI.

4.5.2.3 Improved ad performance:

- ✓ Identifying underperforming ads is just as important as recognizing successes.

- ✓ Once identified, we can examine the reasons for their underperformance and implement targeted improvements.
- ✓ Continuous monitoring and adjustments based on performance data ensure that our ads remain relevant and effective.

4.5.2.4 Deduction

We began this analytical journey by first delineating the tools and libraries essential to our showcase. Next, we selected a dataset that would serve as the foundation for training our machine learning model. With the dataset selected, we proceeded to process and prepare the data, ensuring that it was ready for the next steps. Our next action was to select an appropriate model tailored to our specific needs. Having finalized this choice, we trained our model, which resulted in a commendable accuracy rate of 82%, reflecting the effectiveness of our approach.

To sum up, we successfully presented the following elements:

- ✓ Selecting the right machine learning algorithm for a specific problem;
- ✓ The process of preparing and partitioning data for training and testing ;
- ✓ The measurement, performance and model accuracy of machine learning.

4.6 Conclusion

At the end of this in-depth exploration, we have demonstrated the power of integrating machine learning into digital marketing strategies, particularly in predicting clicks on online ads. This chapter has traced each crucial step in this process, from initial foundations to final implementation.

We began by assembling a set of essential tools and libraries, such as Python, Pandas, NumPy, Matplotlib and Scikit-learn, forming a solid foundation for our book. Next, we carried out careful data preparation, exploring the AVAZU dataset and applying processing techniques to ensure the quality and integrity of our information.

The next phase was to build and train our machine learning model. We carefully selected the logistic regression algorithm, due to its ability to efficiently handle binary classification problems such as click prediction. After dividing our data into training and test sets, we trained our model, which achieved a remarkable accuracy of 82%.

This impressive performance underlines the added value that machine learning can bring to digital marketing strategies. By leveraging the insights gained from our model, companies can optimize their advertising campaigns, maximize revenues and improve the overall performance of their ads. This approach offers a valuable competitive advantage, enabling brands to connect with their target audience in a more relevant and effective way.

Although this chapter has focused on a specific use case, the principles and techniques presented here can be applied to other areas of digital marketing. Machine learning offers vast potential for improving recommendation systems, customer segmentation, sentiment analysis and many other crucial aspects of today's marketing landscape.

In conclusion, this chapter has convincingly demonstrated that integrating machine learning into digital marketing is not just a possibility, but a necessity for companies keen to remain competitive in an ever-changing environment. By embracing this transformative synergy, brands can harness the power of data and artificial intelligence to deliver exceptional customer experiences, foster engagement and, ultimately, drive long-term growth and success.

GENERAL CONCLUSION

This book has explored in depth the revolutionary intersection between digital marketing and machine learning, highlighting the powerful synergies that emerge when these two forces are strategically combined. Our in-depth analysis has traced the historical evolution of these disciplines, deconstructed their different approaches, and highlighted their respective strengths and weaknesses.

We have demonstrated the added value that machine learning can bring to marketing strategies, enabling unprecedented hyper-personalization of interactions, deep customer engagement via innovative channels, and fine-tuning of campaign performance. However, beyond these promising benefits, our study highlights the crucial importance of adopting a measured and nuanced approach.

While machine learning offers immense opportunities, it also carries potential risks such as the echo chamber effect limiting discovery, and the drift towards an artificial online environment eroding consumer trust. The challenge is to find a balance between harnessing this technology wisely, while preserving an authentic link with their target audience.

Ethical and responsible integration of machine learning will be essential to maintaining lasting relationships between brands and consumers. The wisest companies will recognize that AI is only a tool amplifying, not replacing, human marketing expertise. They will embrace this nuance, leveraging the revolutionary potential of machine learning while preserving the soul and authenticity of their brands.

While this book has focused on some specific use cases, the principles and techniques explored can be applied to multiple aspects of digital marketing. By wisely harnessing this transformative synergy, companies can leverage the power of data and AI to deliver exceptional customer experiences, boost engagement, optimize performance, and drive sustainable growth, while respecting core values of authenticity and trust.

BIBLIOGRAPHY

[1] David L. P., Alan K. M. (2023), "Artificial Intelligence: Foundations of Computational Agents", "1.1 what is artificial intelligence?", 3rd edition. https://artint.info/3e/html/ArtInt3e.Ch1.S1.html

[2] David L. P., Alan K. M. (2023), "Artificial Intelligence: Foundations of Computational Agents", "1.4 Prototypical Applications", 3rd edition. https://artint.info/3e/html/ArtInt3e.Ch1.S4.html

[3] Zoe L. (Nov 16, 2022). "General AI vs Narrow AI" https://levity.ai/blog/general-ai-vs-narrow-ai

[4] Selmer B. (Jul 12, 2018), "Artificial Intelligence", "8. Philosophy of Artificial Intelligence". https://plato.stanford.edu/entries/artificial-intelligence/#StroVersWeakAI

[5] Data Camp (May 2023). "What is symbolic AI?". https://www.datacamp.com/blog/what-is-symbolic-ai

[6] Selmer B. (Jul 12, 2018), "Artificial Intelligence", "4.1 Bloom in machine learning". https://plato.stanford.edu/entries/artificial-intelligence/#BlooMachLear

[7] Coursera Staff, (March 27, 2024), "What is Machine Learning? Definition, Types and Examples". https://www.coursera.org/articles/what-is-machine-learning

[8] Nailman A. (August 24, 2023), "The Evolution of Machine Learning: A Brief History and Timeline." https://machinelearningmodels.org/the-evolution-of-machine-learning-a-brief-history-and-timeline/

[9] Anushka J. (29 Nov 2023), "Types Of Machine Learning". https://www.geeksforgeeks.org/types-of-machine-learning/

[10] Robert J. (Jul 31, 2023), "Reinforcement learning: definition and application". https://datascientest.com/reinforcement-learning

[11] Ngaleu A. K. (Jul 4, 2022), "Deep Learning: Definition, concepts and examples". https://datascientest.com/reinforcement-learning

[12] Google, (Jul 31, 2023), "Neural Networks: Structure". https://developers.google.com/machine-learning/crash-course/introduction-to-neural-networks/anatomy

[13] Novak j. (Feb 16, 2024), "What is digital marketing? Types, Strategies, & Best Practices". https://www.forbes.com/advisor/business/what-is-digital-marketing/

[14] Chantrel F. (Oct 28, 2019), "the first banner ad celebrates 25 years". https://www.blogdumoderateur.com/premiere-banniere-pub/

[15] Chris A. (Feb 25, 2024), "12 Types Of Digital Marketing [And How They Work]." https://www.reliablesoft.net/types-of-digital-marketing/

[16] Ryan D.,Russ H. (July 31, 2023), "Digital Marketing For Dummies", 2nd edition, page 263.

[17] Ryan D.,Russ H. (July 31, 2023), "Digital Marketing For Dummies", 2nd edition, page 321.

[18] Hyup Y., (31 Jul 2023), "Hands-on data science for marketing: improve your marketing strategies with machine learning using Python and R",1st edition, page 71.

[19] Andrea De M., Andrea S., Andrea Ba. (June 24, 2022), "Machine learning and artificial intelligence use in marketing: a general taxonomy." https://link.springer.com/article/10.1007/s43039-022-00057-w

[20] Berg A., Provins S., Silberman G., White K., (31 May 2021), "artificial intelligence and echo chambers". https://www.counterterrorismgroup.com/post/artificial-intelligence-and-echo-chambers

[21] Butler S. (Mar 8, 2024), "What Is the Dead Internet Theory?". https://www.howtogeek.com/what-is-the-dead-internet-theory/

[22] Arranz M. I. (Mar 12, 2024), "Data science library hub". https://github.com/imarranz/data-science-library-hub

[23] Wang S., Cukierski W. (2014), "Click-Through Rate Prediction." https://kaggle.com/competitions/avazu-ctr-prediction

MIX
Papier aus verantwortungsvollen Quellen
Paper from responsible sources
FSC® C105338

Printed by Books on Demand GmbH, Norderstedt / Germany